Robert Williamson

CALLED TO PIONEER

Visit us on the Internet
www.kando-verlag.de

Cover design: Marii Brédard
A fish eagle ('Nkwazi') – the national bird of Zambia – against a background of the Victoria Falls or 'Mosi-oa-Tunya' (the Smoke that Thunders). These spectacular falls are located on the Zambezi River at the Zambia-Zimbabwe border.

Printing and binding: Verlag T. Lindemann, Offenbach am Main
ISBN: 978-3-922947-77-6
Printed in Germany

Dedication

To God, Our Heavenly Parent and to my spiritual guides, Reverend and Mrs. Moon, the True Parents of Heaven and Earth and all Humankind.

To my spiritual father Eric Holt. Eric was witnessed to by June Darby-Perrin, the pioneer missionary to Scotland and was the first Scotsman to join in his native country. He in turn witnessed to me on a spring day in March 1972 in Edinburgh, Scotland.

To my eternal beloved wife, Heidrun, given to me by Heaven, who has patiently put up with me and borne our five beautiful children.

To all my leaders and brothers and sisters in faith who over the years have guided my spiritual growth.

To all friends who have contributed to this memoir.

A special mention to my editor Catriona Valenta, who has organised my words into something readable and coherent; to David Fraser-Harris for the professional proof reading and to Thomas Cromwell for his advice and foreword and to my niece Marii Brédard for her creative cover design.

Contents

Introduction

The book you have in your hands is the story of my spiritual journey.

I have written this testimony of my life of faith and experiences with True Parents[1] in the hope that you, the reader, regardless of where you are on your spiritual journey, may be inspired to (re)discover God, our Heavenly Parent[2] and how He desires to work in your life.

Although I first encountered my spiritual guides, True Parents, at the age of nineteen, my searching began much earlier. I have always believed that life is not just about eating, sleeping, and working, but that our existence has an internal purpose. Most of us develop self-awareness at the age of about four or five (at least in my case, my memory extends to this point) and spend the rest of our lives searching for purpose and meaning. Our course usually takes us through formal education - independence from parents - employment and earning a living - partnership and marriage - raising a family. But we often cannot find answers to basic questions such as: *Is there a God? What is the origin of the universe and mankind? What is behind all the faith stories? Has there*

---

[1] True Parents – the name given to the Founders of the Holy Spirit Association for World Christianity (HSA-UWC), now known as the Family Federation for World Peace (FFWPU), Reverend Sun Myung Moon and Dr. Hak Ja Han Moon

[2] Heavenly Parent – the name given to God in Unification Theology

been any meaning and direction to history? Is this life all there is, or is there life after death? What is true love? So many questions and we spend our lives trying to find answers!

I was fortunate in that my encounter with Eric Holt in 1972 brought for me answers to many of these questions. But that was only a stage in the journey. Every day brings a new discovery.

Now that I'm in my sixties, time seems to march past at an incredible pace. It was not always so; when I was fifteen, time stretched out endlessly. I scratched off each day in my diary at boarding school and it seemed to take so long to reach the far-distant end of term.

We might prefer to deny or ignore our vanishing muscles and the alarmingly rapid development of wrinkles, but the mirror tells no lies. Eyesight deteriorates as does hearing. Why is everybody nagging me to invest in a hearing aid? What did my mother say about no one thinking they are getting old?

And so, the time has come, before my memory advances too far along the path of deterioration, to set down in writing my legacy – my life of faith. Perhaps you will be intrigued by my story and be inspired on your own spiritual journey.

Foreword
by Thomas Cromwell

Religion is difficult to understand from the outside. Why would a monk give up the pleasures of life to devote himself to prayer and service? Why would he trade comforts we all cherish for a life in a small, austere cell, sleeping and eating just enough to sustain himself? Why would a nun travel to a distant land to serve the poor and the sick, giving up the warmth of a family home and the deep satisfaction of motherhood? And why would devout believers be willing to suffer torture and death rather than betray their faith, or immolate themselves to protest injustice?

Robert Williamson's story is not about life in a monk's cell or Communist prison, but it is a story of faith in difficult times and under difficult circumstances. The Unification Church, which he joined as a young man, was always controversial. Its Korean founder, Sun Myung Moon, taught a radical interpretation of the Bible and was generally despised and rejected by mainstream Christian churches. His followers were all too often the target of ridicule. They were labelled brainwashed heretics and rejected by their families and communities. It took courage and strong faith to persevere.

Robert's testimony provides an insight into one person's life of faith within the Unification Church, beginning in Scotland, moving to America, then to Zambia (his place of birth), Cote d'Ivoire, Russia, Southeast Europe and finally back to Africa. Life in the Church was never easy. Most of its leaders came from Korea or Japan, and cultural differences were always challenging. And opposition from outside the Church always made the work particularly difficult.

Membership in the Church is truly international, and one of the enriching benefits of Robert's life was working with people of all backgrounds. As a life-long missionary, learning to live and work with diverse people was never easy. It required that he go beneath the surface of colour and culture to build an authentic community. For a missionary, diversity can never be an excuse for failure; it is your mission to overcome profound differences for the sake of building God's Kingdom of Heaven on earth.

Robert has been a loyal friend since we first met in America in the early 1970s. Our paths have crisscrossed over the years, but he has always been constant. He could have lived a comfortable life in Scotland, but he chose differently. This is the story of his life of faith. Through it you can come to understand the pull of Unificationist belief, why this particular person was moved by this particular religion to devote his life to God's service. For those who seek a deeper understanding of God and the Unification religion, this is a valuable and important book.

How It All Began

Edinburgh, 31 March 1972

I must have looked like many a young man of the time – a bearded, long-haired youth wearing a long grey coat – as I walked along Princes Street, one of the most beautiful and famous streets in Europe.

But was there something about me that betrayed the fact that I was a spiritual seeker – that I had attended spiritual meetings and seances? Why did a young man suddenly appear in front of me, and ask if I was 'interested in spiritual things?'

I, a student of Hotel Management at Napier College, Edinburgh was about to embark on a life of discipleship in the Unified Family of True Parents.

But my story really started almost twenty years before that.

Chapter One:
Childhood

Northern Rhodesia, 15 April 1952

In 1952, Great Britain was mourning the death of King George VI and welcoming the young Queen Elizabeth as his successor. In those days, Great Britain was a nation which still had a vast empire and many colonies. One such colony was the African country of Northern Rhodesia, now known as Zambia. This is where I was born in April 1952, to a Scottish engineer in the copper mines and his wife, a nurse in the mining hospital.

Although Northern Rhodesia/Zambia was to later play a pivotal role in my life, my initial stay was short; when I was two years old, my family moved to northern Ontario in Canada, to the small gold mining town of Pamour, just outside the larger town of Timmins.

This is where I started my schooling, at Pamour primary and was first introduced to sport. And what an introduction! Ice hockey was and still is serious business in Canada; children are put into skates as soon as they can walk, and I have clear memories of playing ice hockey for the local maple leaf peewee team. I remember when the puck hit one of my friends straight on his nose; despite the prompt first aid administered by my mother, the ice turned bright crimson!

1950, My parents (Bob & Marie) on their wedding day Luanshya Zambia (Northern Rhodesia).

Left: Age 2. Right: 1956, aged 4 in Canada with my sister Fiona.

During those years I had my first spiritual experience. I remember when I was about six or seven, seeing a bright light out of the corner of my eye whilst sitting at home. What was it? I do not know. But from that time on, I thought there was something beyond that which is visible, and I became interested in God and spiritual matters and always very curious about the bigger unseen world around us.

In 1959 we moved back to Northern Rhodesia to re-join the mining fraternity in a small town called Mufulira. I was first enrolled into the local Convent School and then, at the age of ten, was sent to the local boarding school in Kitwe, St. Francis College.

My memories of that time are of wonderful family barbecues during vacations, of learning to play football and of my academic and general knowledge lessons at boarding school.

Although I was technically a Protestant, the boarding school was Catholic and I was introduced to the Catholic format of mass, or Sunday service. Our misdemeanours rarely escaped the eagle-eyes of the Brothers and discipline was never far away. One Sunday we had to fast, missing breakfast because the Brothers claimed that somebody had let off a rude noise, considered disruptive to the holy atmosphere!

I remember at least once getting lashings from a sjambok, a rhinoceros hide short whip, for causing a disturbance in class. This was administered on the backside and was either three or six strokes depending on the crime. The result was painful welts, but no tears could be shed in front of my friends – because that would not be manly.

And on reflection, some things were rather odd for a Catholic boarding school, for example the occasional Saturday evening showings of Dracula movies. For a ten-year-old this was scary stuff: I often hid behind the chair in front of me as I tried to figure out what was going on.

But I also have good memories of feeling safe and secure, snuggling down in my bed to the sound of crickets and the African night noises, and looking out the window at the huge sky full of twinkling stars.

The days drifted into months and then a couple of years passed, and in 1964 I was sent to Scotland with my mother. I was to prepare for my entrance exam to Merchiston Castle School in Edinburgh, which I entered in 1965.

Merchiston Castle, the oldest public school in Scotland, was founded by Charles Chalmers in 1833 at the original Merchiston house building in Morningside, Edinburgh and moved to its present location in 1930. This school with its motto of 'ready, aye ready' was my home for five years.

I have fond memories of lots of study, sports and extra-curricular activities at Merchiston. But two experiences were especially significant.

Firstly, I joined the Christian Club where we studied the Bible and prayed, and where I gave my life to Jesus. But nothing seemed to happen. I would pray and study and have all sorts of questions, but always received the same answer: *"Well, you must pray about it."* Perhaps my expectations were simply too great. Maybe I was expecting some sort of direct conversation with Jesus and the saints, but nothing seemed to happen and so I continued to drift along spiritually without any real conviction in my belief.

The second experience was a séance which was organised by me and three of my friends. We duly constructed a Ouija board, and all four of us put our index fingers on an upside-down glass; the glass started to move all over the board.

1970, Captain of athletics team Merchiston Castle School (front row centre).

We then asked what I suppose was the spirit, some dates of battles – and sure enough, the dates were correct! At this stage, the whole experience became overwhelming and suddenly one of my friends started trembling as if possessed; we threw the board up in the air and that was the end of that. In hindsight, my friend was probably spiritually open, and although I have no idea what was going on, the experiment ended abruptly and was not repeated.

I graduated and left Merchiston in 1970 and enrolled in Napier College, Edinburgh as a student of Hotel Management. My life journey and spiritual search continued. The decade before, the 'swinging sixties', had resulted in a decline in moral standards. This was the time of free-love, free spirits, endless pop music and parties where the air was heavy with 'pot'. My avocation as an athlete (I was a 400-metres sprinter for my school) protected me, or at least gave me the excuse I needed when offered a smoke – I just pretended to inhale.

During this time, I dated a girl quite seriously and although we were only eighteen, we could often meet up as I had my own small apartment. We had highs and lows and I was often consumed with jealousy because she had had a previous boyfriend. This led to arguments; I could have girlfriends, but she should have no others in her life. And I always felt there was something missing and that we did not have permission from God to have a physical relationship.

Despite all this freedom, I experienced a deep internal loneliness, and only later did I realise this to be a spiritual loneliness and that void needed to be filled with the love of God, my Heavenly Father and Parent.

I knew there was something out there. I just wanted to find out answers to my questions. Basic questions such as: *What is the meaning of life? Is there life after death? What was the mission of Jesus? Why is there so much pain and suffering in the world? Why is there so much contradiction?* and many more.

And so perhaps it was no wonder that I was approached in Princes Street Edinburgh by the young man who asked me if I was 'interested in spiritual things?'

Chapter Two: A Student Becomes a Disciple of True Parents

'Spiritual things?' – I had hardly time to answer in the affirmative and take the pamphlet he thrust into my hand, before the young man, Eric Holt, disappeared.

My curiosity and interest awakened, I persuaded two Christian friends to accompany me to the address on the leaflet – a flat in quite a respectable area of Edinburgh – for a Wednesday evening lecture.

I remember the thumping of my heart, the mixture of emotions, and the strikingly blue eyes of the tall lady who opened the door. In retrospect, I am fairly certain that she had been fasting.

We were ushered in and offered seats in front of a chalk board on which, with the help of a few simple diagrams, our hostess taught us the essence of chapter one of the Divine Principle, using what was known as the 'red book', a version by Young Oon Kim.[3] It was so simple and 'obvious', and I really wanted to know what came next. On the second day we returned and heard about the Fall of Man: this profound truth deeply moved me but my Christian friends were not

[3] Young Oon Kim (1914-1989), leading church theologian and first missionary to the United States

impressed, and so on the third day I returned alone. After that there was no going back.

On the suggestion of Eric, I attended a workshop in England and fasted for three days; on the third day of my fast, Eric helped me pack my few belongings.

One month after my first visit, I moved into that top floor flat in Edinburgh. The tall lady, June Darby-Perrin, was my first centre leader. The atmosphere in the centre was wonderful. After a full day at college, I gathered with the others in the evening for a simple meal. We would share and reflect together about our day and then prepare the lounge for the evening lecture, which was taught by each of us in turn. Our days always ended with prayer.

Early on, when it was my turn to pray, I entered a trance-like state in which my own spirit seemed to move aside and make room for the spirit of God to speak through me. I had no control over what I was saying but heard myself talking about the Second Coming of the Messiah, an end to conflict, Rev. Moon and much more. Suddenly I returned to my normal state and began to weep uncontrollably. When I asked the others what had happened, June casually responded that I had just had a 'special experience', but that there was no cause for concern. A less dramatic form of that experience occurred the following evening but has never since been repeated. Over the years when faced with struggles or difficulties, I have always returned to, and gained strength from, this first spiritual experience.

I had been in the centre for no longer than one week when June announced that we were to go out witnessing. On this occasion that meant public speaking. I had always wondered why there was a little box in the corner of the kitchen. That Sunday I was to find out!

Our brave little group of four made its way to 'Speakers' Corner' near the Princes Street Art Gallery. I carried the box. June was the first; she jumped on the little box and started loudly proclaiming the Principle of Creation - the first chapter of Reverend Moon's revelation, 'the Divine Principle'. Then came my turn. I was a novice and was trembling like a leaf, but 'if the centre leader needs this to be done, I had better go for it'. And so, I went for it. I leapt onto the box and started shouting about the Fall of Man. Was anybody stopping? No.

Maybe I had to shout louder. I increased the volume and on noticing that a couple of people had stopped to listen, I became even more passionate and enthusiastic. After several more minutes I became completely hoarse and lost my voice, and it was the turn of the others. Did anybody follow us back to the centre for a lecture? No. But this was my training! That was my introduction to public speaking and public mission – baptism by sweat rather than fire, so to speak. Over the following weeks and months, I learnt how to project my voice, keep calm, make eye contact, and engage the audience.

I was full of hope, passion, and energy to spread the truth. To assist our outreach efforts, we 'set indemnity conditions'. This entails denial of the body through strong measures such as fasting or cold baths, to 'set a condition' for spiritual assistance, in this case to guide us to people prepared to hear the message. I have vivid memories of plunging into a bath of icy water, counting to forty, and then leaping out completely pink and trembling!

Flushed with enthusiasm and naivety, I expected that the whole world would easily understand and accept the message of Rev. Moon. I was still attending college and witnessed to all my friends, some of whom came to the centre and listened to the teachings. But only one, Oliver Lane, joined. He was in the class above me. Also, Fiona, my sister who had just finished boarding school in England, joined our group in Edinburgh after having attended a workshop. But by the end of 1972 we were still only a handful of members: Eric, the first Scottish member who witnessed to me; I brought Oliver and Fiona; Fiona witnessed to Hamish Robertson outside the Princes Street art gallery; Elizabeth Bateson joined in Glasgow.

Left: 1972, aged 19 just before meeting the church in Edinburgh, Scotland. Right: Circa 1982, with Eric Holt who introduced me to the movement 10 years earlier.

After much discussion, Oliver and I decided to drop out of college and dedicate ourselves as full-time volunteers. I decided to complete my first year so that my parents would know that I was not leaving because of failure to make the grades, but because I had found my calling in life. My parents were not pleased; they were still living in Zambia and Fiona and I flew out to teach them the Principle and explain our decision. They dutifully listened as we read them the Principle. If they perhaps imagined and hoped that we would grow out of this phase and come to our senses, they must have been disappointed!

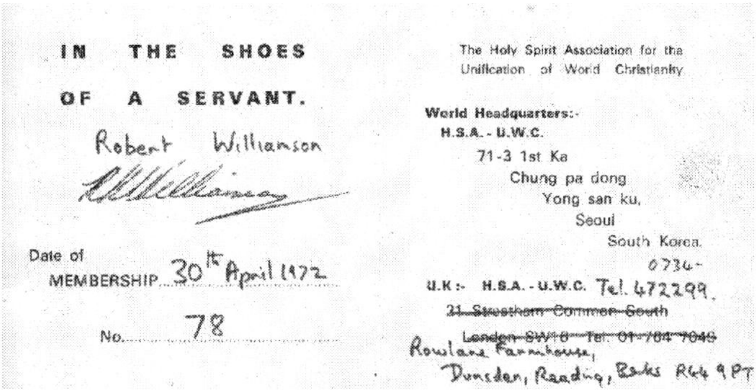
IN THE SHOES OF A SERVANT.

Robert Williamson

Date of MEMBERSHIP 30th April 1972

No. 78

The Holy Spirit Association for the Unification of World Christianity

World Headquarters:-
H.S.A.-U.W.C.
71-3 1st Ka
Chung pa dong
Yong san ku,
Seoul
South Korea.

U.K:- H.S.A.-U.W.C. Tel. 0734-472299.
~~31 Streatham Common South~~
~~London SW16 Tel: 01-764 7046~~
Rowlane Farmhouse,
Dunsden, Reading, Berks RG4 9PT

1972, first membership card UK.

On my return to the UK, Dennis and Doris Orme, the then national leaders, asked me to join the legendary 'Samson' mobile fundraising team (MFT) of ten brothers. No-one could miss Samson, a massive converted furniture van, its sides decorated with a Bible verse about the Messiah's return. In Samson we travelled around the country and sold on the street, for about 20 pence each, magazines containing chapters of the Divine Principle. This was my introduction to fundraising.

We estimated that perhaps every fifth person would buy and so our tactic was to approach as many people as possible. At that time in 1972, we raised a daily average of about £15, but each day we challenged an increasingly higher goal. I remember the great day when some of us broke through the £20 barrier. We celebrated with an extra portion of sausage goulash on our primus stove in the furniture van!

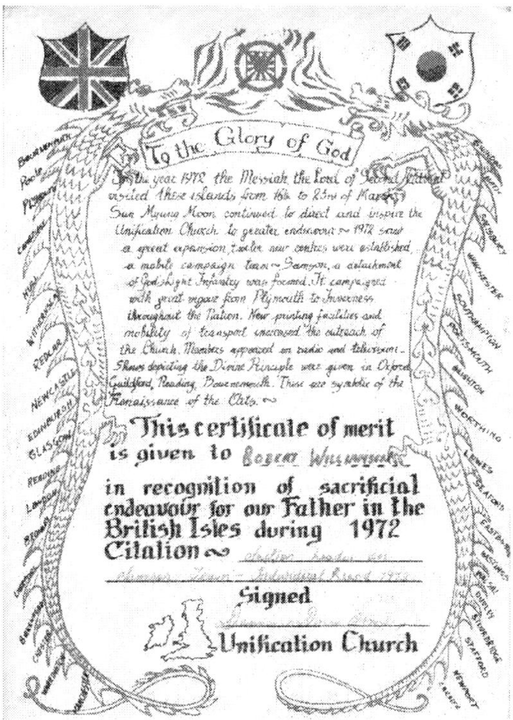
To the Glory of God

In the year 1972 the Messiah the Lord of [illegible] visited these islands from [illegible] to 23rd of March. Sun Myung Moon continued to direct and inspire the Unification Church to greater endeavour ~ 1972 saw a great expansion, twelve new centres were established, a mobile campaign team ~ Samson, a detachment of God's Light Infantry was formed. It campaigned with great vigour from Plymouth to Inverness throughout the Nation. New printing facilities and mobility of transport increased the outreach of the Church. Members appeared on radio and television. Shows depicting the Divine Principle were given in Oxford, Guildford, Reading, Bournemouth. These are symbolic of the Renaissance of the Celts. ~

This certificate of merit is given to [illegible]

in recognition of sacrificial endeavour for our Father in the British Isles during 1972

Citation ~ [illegible]

Signed [illegible]

Unification Church

1972, individual fundraising record.

Chapter Three:
A Missionary in America

Rev. Moon arrived in the United States of America at the end of 1971. He realised that winning this great country for God was a vital step towards influencing the whole world. In January 1973, Dennis and Doris Orme, the then national leaders of the UK, were asked by True Father to send around a dozen members to assist the pioneer work in America. Although we had been church members for less than a year, my sister Fiona and I were assigned to that first team.

The anticipatory excitement was overwhelming, and I well remember all of us praying fervently in the rear of the plane in preparation for the great new mission.

Our flight from London arrived at JFK International Airport New York. We collected our bags and made our way to the arrivals area. Suddenly somebody whispered that True Father had come to meet us! Sure enough, there were Father and Mother with their closest assistants, scrutinizing us intently and greeting us with beaming smiles. This was my first encounter with the Messiah!

Before we knew it, we were on the bus, heading into New York, all talking at once. "*Did you see True Father?*" "*Incredible – isn't it wonderful that True Father came to meet us!*" As a foundation for our mission in America, we were to first attend a forty-day workshop, held in Belvedere estate in New York's Hudson Valley.

Belvedere had just been bought the previous year with funds raised from the selling of candles and flowers by dedicated and hard-working American members.

Various church elders were allocated as lecturers, one of whom was Papa-san Choi, an early Korean member sent by True Father in the mid-1960s to pioneer the west coast of America. True Father himself would talk to us for hours and hours. After each session, the chalkboard was covered, and the floor coated with chalk. We would rush to the board to pick up a souvenir piece of chalk which Father had directly used. David SC Kim, also sent by True Father in the late 1950s to pioneer America, was the main translator.

I learned that one must be really prepared before listening to True Father because his speeches were guided by inspiration and not the clock. But once you had got your place, the last thing you wanted to do was leave – not even for the bathroom! It seems like only yesterday that I was listening to Father so energetically teaching and explaining things to us. It was as if we were mesmerised; his words transfixed me and kept me glued to my seat.

I had been asked by Dennis and Doris to lead the British team. This did not involve much more than simply keeping an eye on everyone and ensuring that all were coping well with the schedule. True Father was greatly concerned about our well-being and I remember him touring the dormitories, making sure that the beds were satisfactory and that we were comfortable.

At the end of the forty days, True Father gathered us all together and we had to line up as he chose prospective leaders. I silently vowed: "*Father if you choose me, I will really do my best*" – and then suddenly True Father pointed at me and put me in the front along with a few others. He then assigned all the European members to teams, and I found myself leader of ten Europeans. Father then did one of his famous 'spiritual lotteries' and we were assigned to Florida, which had been designated as the centre of several states in the South East region. I was to understudy my American counterpart Jon Schuhart, and after four or five months we would be reassigned.

A journey of almost one thousand miles from New York to Florida lay ahead of us.

In those days, the ten-seater automatic Dodge van, an amazingly comfortable vehicle with a large gas-guzzling engine, was almost universally used as the mode of transport in our movement. Our driver from the south-east was Bob Heater, a great brother with a terrific sense of humour who considered our accents to be '*really neat*'.

January 1973, our team to pioneer Florida after training at Belvedere USA with our Founders.

We arrived after a day or two to find a team of our American counterparts – also about ten in number, brothers, and sisters – in the middle of their prayer.

"Robert they are praying in a circle and they are all holding hands!" This sister expressed our collective horror. We had been raised in a strict atmosphere in Europe where the rules were: no touching, no looking and certainly no holding hands with the opposite sex! It was a strict brother and sister relationship. What was I to do?

"I do not know the traditions here in America, but we must fit in so let us just join the circle."

And so, with great trepidation we were introduced to the American way of working as a family, where everyone took responsibility to maintain relationships on the level of brother and sister and keep any other emotions in check. The next two years were spent pioneering Florida and the neighbouring states.

November 1973, our Founder buying souvenirs for members at Cape Canaveral Space Force Station, Florida with Jutta and me.

Rev. Moon embarked on several speaking tours to bring God's message to the USA, and in 1973 he visited Tampa, Florida on his 'Day of Hope' campaign. This was indeed a highlight for us; True Parents stayed in our small centre of less than ten members. In the evening, True Father spoke at a public event on the theme of 'Christianity in Crisis' and during the day he toured some of the local sites such as Cape Canaveral and the Tampa Bay area. True Parents' stay with us was indeed a very historic and memorable occasion. Several other notable figures in our early movement accompanied Father: Mrs. Won Bok Choi, David S.C. Kim, Colonel Pak and Daikon, True Father's driver.

November 1973, our Founder speaking on his 'Christianity in Crisis' tour, Tampa, Florida. Welcoming dinner, left to right Mrs. Choi, Reverend Moon, Neil Salonen, Charles Anceney, me, Mrs. Moon, Dr. Pak.

One morning David Kim's voice boomed from upstairs: "*Who polished Father's shoes?*" I exchanged sheepish glances with another brother. David Kim told us never to untie the shoelaces because True Father always used a shoe-horn to save valuable seconds.

November 1973, visiting Disneyland, Florida with our Founders and Dr. Kim, Dr. Pak, Mrs. Choi & Lady Dr. Kim.

This taught us how precious time is to True Father; not even one second was to be lost or wasted. On our trip to Cape Canaveral, I was driving the lead car, and I asked Daikon how fast we should go. His answer: "*Just fast!*" with the goal of not being overtaken. True Father also loved McDonalds because of the speed of service, and this is where we lunched on the way back to the centre.

In later years, such closely shared times with True Parents became less common; how fortunate we were then! How precious to share meals, to sing a song at the dinner table and be such an intimate part of True Parents' family.

1974, appointed as state leader of Florida.

My age made me ineligible by only a few months for the 1800 couples Blessing[4] in February 1975. From this Blessing group, missionaries were assigned to pioneer the church on an international level. On learning from Mr. Salonen, our national director that nobody had yet been assigned to Zambia, I volunteered to represent America and go to my country of birth. He obtained Father's permission and thus I attended a 100-day missionary preparation workshop in the seminary in Barrytown, NY.

[4] Blessing - name given to the mass wedding ceremony of the church.

On 30 April 1975 I departed from JFK airport for Zambia, armed with a small Bible – a gift from the American Church – my Divine Principle book, some Holy Salt to sanctify things (similar to the use of holy water in other faiths), some soil to make a Holy Prayer ground, a few dollars in my pocket and great excitement in my heart.

Chapter Four:
Missionary to Zambia

The early years

I was a young teenager when in early 1964 I left Northern Rhodesia to continue my schooling. Just a few months later, in October 1964, the nation gained independence and became Zambia. Now it was 1975 and here I was again, returning as an idealistic missionary and disciple of True Parents! And how could I have known then that another fifteen years would pass before I would leave Zambia as a family man with a wife and children?

Many of the members who were sent out as missionaries in 1975 – at least those from the West – were young in more ways than one. On 1 May 1975 when I arrived in Zambia, I was just twenty-three years old; and I had been a member of the Unification Church for a mere three years. The entry in my diary on that momentous day was short and to the point:

1 May 1975: Arrived today, Thursday. Got a taxi to the Hotel in Lusaka and checked into a single room for 15 kwacha a day! (I do not think I was aware of the money problem at this stage as I tipped heavily). *It was also Labour Day – embassies closed – went and walked around Lusaka Club* (where I used to play squash as a teenager in the late 60's*) – didn't see the 'old gang'. I think I recognised one girl, but do not know her name.*

April 1975, missionaries sent to Africa from the USA with our Founder & children at Unification Church Seminary USA after training (I am 5th from the right back row).

To each mission country representatives were sent out from three nations – Japan, Germany, and the USA (as mentioned, I represented the USA). In order to find each other, we had left messages at each other's embassies. Rudolf (Germany) and I found each other quickly.

2 May 1975: Had my previous night's prayer answered and met Rudolf Faerber from Germany. Discovered his message at the American Embassy. He was staying in a dingy flat at Nightingale Court. Had supper in the hotel on top of my suitcase: peanuts, bread and cheese, marmite. Also went and saw Mr. Banda briefly about becoming a Zambian citizen – lost it (citizenship) in 1973; must write a letter of appeal.

3 May 1975: Met Rudolf in the morning and sent a telegram to the USA for ginseng tea papers. Had our first unity argument about buying food! Met Mr. & Mrs. Shick and got (leave) house in Kalundu for a month only to pay Paul the housekeeper 48 kwacha a month – $76! Also 3 cats there. The Shicks met us in the evening and were shocked to taste ginseng tea! 'Leave houses' were the homes of the many British expatriates in Lusaka. When they returned to Britain, they needed someone to look after their house. This was an absolute godsend for us because it meant living rent-free in return for the responsibility of taking care of the house, any staff and pets. We could stay in a good, secure environment and save our missionary allowance (about $200 per month, sent by our respective nations).

8 May 1975: Still no sign of Japanese brother. Saw President Kaunda returned from the USA – stood on Great East Road and waved to him – a spiritual condition for the future.

For some reason the Japanese missionary did not get our first messages left at the Japanese Embassy. But eventually, around the middle of May 1975, he turned up at the house where Rudolf and I were staying.

Eiju Majima's English was not so easy to understand, but it was clear that he was so relieved to meet us. Most of his money had been stolen; he was living rough and was very thin. He had already been blessed in marriage on 8 February 1975 but his wife remained in Japan, intending to come to

Zambia when a foundation had been laid. Now we were a team of three.

Rudolf, Majima-san and I quickly established ourselves on the 'leave house circuit' and gained a reputation for being responsible and reliable. Although this meant moving every few months, it was no great hardship as we had few belongings and could live out of one suitcase each.

Circa 1978, myself, Eiju Majima, Rudolf Faerber.

For the first six months, our mode of travel was hitch-hiking. I was experienced and confidently trained the other two: *"Stand on the side of the road – stick your thumb out and look reasonably presentable!"*

It worked well for us; it took an average of thirty minutes to reach downtown Lusaka from the suburb of Kabulonga, we met a lot of people to whom we could witness, and we saved money!

Many of the 'leave houses' had vegetable gardens and fruit trees, and we supplemented these basics with eggs, milk and the occasional piece of meat and thus could eat quite well. But this was not so at the very beginning; I remember hanging up a tea bag to dry so that it could provide our brews for a couple of days!

It was certainly challenging in many ways for our different cultures to harmonise. Even eating together was a challenge: "*Majima-san, why do you make so much noise when you eat – you sound like a farmyard.*"

I was to learn that in the orient if you make noise, it means that you are really enjoying the meal!

Majima-san to me: "*Why do you keep bothering me asking to pass you the salt and pepper? Why don't you get it yourself?*" I had to explain to him that where I grew up, it was considered rude to stretch over the table.

The fact that we had three different native languages also added to our challenges. We chose to communicate in English as Zambia is a former British colony.

As time went on, we found a happy medium, could communicate better and tolerate the different cultural quirks! From the start we made a big effort to reach out to the Christian Anglican community. We attended services at the Anglican cathedral, met the congregation socially and became involved in activities such as the church fete. We also organised a youth service and even increased the attendance from ten to forty-five! But since the community members were mostly expatriates and very set in their beliefs, they were not so open to the ideas we had to share.

I was aware that a successful sports project had been initiated by one of our members, Glenda Moody, to help disadvantaged black American youth in the suburbs of Washington, DC, and I was inspired to use this method to approach the Zambian youth. Thus the 'Lusaka Striders Club' came into being.

These excerpts from letters which I wrote to Church Headquarters in July 1975 give some insight into the development of this project:

7 July 1975: We have started the Lusaka Striders Club, patterned after the famous D. C. Striders of Washington, D.C., an inner-city track team famous for its procurement of college athletic scholarships for its members and for its record-breaking performances. We have our first training and timing on Friday. I saw the dean of students at the Zambia University and he is very enthusiastic about our scheme and has given us full use of the university track and facilities. Now we are finding the athletes!

4 August 1975: Our Japanese missionary and I went up to northern Zambia on Saturday by train (one way; we hitch-hiked back!) and met the secretary of the Zambia Amateur Athletics Association about the Lusaka Striders Club. We talked a few minutes, and he is processing our constitution.... We have found the club to be quite a good means of meeting people and building up a relationship. We are hoping to have a match sometime this month. I was happy to see a picture published here of the USA team which set a world relay record, and a couple of them I believe are from the D.C. Striders. The boys were deeply impressed!

26 August 1975: Last week I escorted a Christian Ceylonese girl to a banquet at the Intercontinental Hotel and met some good influential people for the future. One of them was the American counsellor to the embassy, and he knew of our D. C. Striders in Washington. Our Lusaka Striders have been registered with the Zambian Amateur Athletics Association; (other clubs) are a little worried I think at some extra competition. One of our boys recently won the 110-meter hurdles in the Zambian School Championships!

This activity led to my gaining my first 'spiritual children' – George Chipeta and Robert Phiri who in turn witnessed to founding members Casewell Furusa, and Josephine and Beauty Kambikambi.

By the middle of 1978 we had a membership of about twelve.

Laying a financial foundation

Although all foreign missionaries received monetary support from their respective countries, True Father's hope and vision was that a solid financial foundation would be established in each country, allowing independence and freedom to focus on spiritual activities.

We in Zambia were blessed to have developed a business venture which continues to this day – 'Twikatane Farm products'. ('Twikatane' – 'unity' in Bemba, the local language). This exemplary and successful enterprise was born from a fortuitous chat we had one day about sausages. The beginnings are best described in this excerpt from a long article in the April 1980[5] edition of 'Today's World', a church publication with a large international readership:

---

[5] 'Zambian Financial Success Leads to Spiritual Growth – an Interview with Robert Williamson'. George C. Edwards, Today's World, April 1980.

...the impetus for starting the business came from a casual conversation. The subject of sausages happened to come up while they were discussing what kinds of businesses they could start to make money to support themselves. Rudolf's father had once owned a pub in Bavaria. ... his father began to produce his own sausages for sale in the pub. Rudolf thus learned the rudiments of making sausages as a boy in his father's pub. In Zambia he had also met a German man who made sausages on a small scale for sale in the country and who described his work to him.

The next day they purchased some ingredients and got to work... Rudolf's sausages tasted good even though it was his first attempt.

The sausage business got underway in late 1975 under the name of 'Twikatane farm products'.

True Father was so inspired by our sausage factory project that in 1978 he gave us a donation of $20,000. Rudolf went straight to Germany and bought some machinery which was shipped by container to Zambia and I secured a small twenty-acre farm in the Barlastone Park area on the outskirts of Lusaka. We moved there in the autumn of 1978, initially as renters paying about 200 kwacha a month ($180), but after three years the property became our own. This property – Twikatane Farm – still houses the manufacturing plant for the sausage products.

Twikatane Farm also became the first centre established by Eiju Majima, Rudolf Faerber and me, the three original missionaries. We were joined later by Masaki Sasamoto and Uwe Schneider who were unable to stay in their respective original countries, Malawi, and Kenya. Sasamoto-san would later become the first church martyr; he was killed in Tanzania in 1980.

In 1978 I was appointed National Leader of Zambia by Rev Kwak who headed the World Mission Headquarters in New York.

In those days the lines of communication were quite simple and direct and Rev Kwak was the only intermediary between me and True Father. As National Leader I had complete freedom to develop the mission as I saw fit. Our witnessing outreach continued, with each missionary utilising his own special interest and talents. Rudolf worked with his German community contacts, Majima-san with his contacts as a newspaper correspondent and I with my contacts from sporting activities. Sasamoto-san displayed his painting talents by holding exhibitions and Uwe employed his interest in farming and managed the Twikatane piggery for two years. And through our 'sausage factory' we were regularly making contacts.

But there was always a strong spiritual base as a foundation for our external activities. Prayer was an essential element in our lives.

I remember this being explained to me with a story about a cart with two wheels. One wheel represents spiritual matters – witnessing, rallies, workshops and all the activities which grow church membership – and the other represents finances – either business or fundraising. Both are necessary for the cart to go forwards, and if there is imbalance, the cart just goes around and around in circles!

Often those who put their faith in spiritual guidance and assistance appear to others to be crazy. Indeed, anyone passing by the main room in Twikatane on a Sunday morning in those early days may well have considered me to be quite mad. I would set out twelve chairs – which remained empty

– and proceed with a full order of service including song, prayer, and sermon!

But I knew in my heart that such a condition would move those in the spiritual world to send their descendants to us, and so it was. By the beginning of 1980, those chairs were no longer empty; over twelve native Zambian members joined us to live in the centre.

These were young people, most of whom were still attending school and I had to request the permission of their parents before they could live with us. Most were happy that their children would be living with missionaries and have their educational expenses taken care of.

A typical day of life in the centre followed a clear pattern. Morning prayers - breakfast - transport to school with lunch box - day at school - return to centre for dinner - an hour's work in the factory - homework - lights out by 22:00.

During the first five years of our mission in Zambia, we were unavoidably caught up in a war which was raging on our doorstep. Between 1964 and 1980, the neighbouring country of South Rhodesia (now Zimbabwe) was embroiled in the Rhodesian Bush War or Zimbabwe War of Liberation. Many of the freedom fighter groups were based in Zambia, and one of several large training camps was quite near our farm in Lusaka West. Because the Rhodesian air force often crossed the border to bomb these camps, we were subjected to frequent curfews and had to black-out our windows at night with blankets.

It was indeed terrifying and shocking to hear the droning of the bombers overhead, the dull thud of the bombs as they hit the ground, followed by the wails and screams of the casualties. How profoundly tragic is human conflict! Our white skin colour put us at risk of being mistaken for spies, and we had to take great care not to venture too close to a training house. There were occasions when I think that I was saved by the grace of God alone and was able to simply drive off unhindered after being ordered to stop.

1980-1985

In 1980, mission headquarters organised Africa into regions and I was appointed Regional Director of East Africa, which meant I was responsible for Zambia, Zimbabwe, Malawi, Tanzania, Kenya, Uganda, and Somalia. I decided to set up our regional office in Lusaka, Zambia and from there to travel around the region every few months. I visited the members, who updated me on all their projects, while I gave talks and sermons and checked church growth. Fortunately, the financial success of the sausage factory and other projects enabled this frequent travelling.

This was a time when our church was flourishing; there was a great growth in membership and business activities were doing well. I had many memorable experiences during my trips round the region. Two amusing encounters come specially to mind.

Eiju Majima, our Japanese missionary had been appointed national leader of Malawi and I paid him a visit in my capacity as Regional Director. Why did he always switch off his car engine on going downhill; was this another cultural quirk? No – it was: '*to save electricity*!' Neither of us knew much about the workings of a modern automobile engine, but a heated discussion ensued in which each of us tried to justify his opinion!

The only white British missionary in a Moslem country was our own Elizabeth, who had joined in Glasgow; on one of my visits, I was surprised to find a refrigerator in her home stocked almost full of delicacies such as salami. "*Ah yes*", replied the canny Scot, "*a British naval ship docked here for a few days and I persuaded the British Embassy that the naval officers must visit my humble dwelling – hence the few gifts.*" She was a brave woman and even the British embassy was under the spell of this missionary who preached about God and our True Parents.

Circa 1980, town centre Lusaka.

Outreach

These five years were spent expanding the church from the grassroots level and culminated in the second annual 'God Bless Zambia' rally in October 1985. We could gain an associate membership of 10,000, develop an interfaith dialogue amongst the main churches in Lusaka and succeed in media outreach.

1984, Zambian leadership.

I would like to quote from our church article at the time; "*The last speaker was one of our older Zambian brothers, Dannie Nyendwa. Though a junior compared to the stature of the two previous speakers, Dannie was the one quoted by the media for his call to all churches to unite and prepare together to receive the returning Messiah."*

This happened a few months after Reverend Moon's release from Danbury Correction Facility in the USA, where he had been imprisoned on a trumped-up charge of tax evasion, widely recognised as a case of religious and racial persecution. In Zambia we were happy that we could bring some comfort to God's heart over this great injustice by having good church growth at this time.

1986, young team leaders in Zambia.

Chapter Five: The Blessing

I have dedicated a separate chapter to this account of the most momentous episode in my life.

30 December 1980 is a date that will forever be etched in my memory. I was 'matched' with Heidrun.[6]

Even by Unification standards our 'matching' was somewhat unusual; Heidrun was 'matched' to my photograph!

I had just returned to Zambia from America after attending a leaders' conference in New York when I received a telegram. Could I please return immediately to New York as our Founders were going to have a matching ceremony? What was an impoverished missionary to do at such short notice?

Although most of these 'matchings' took place in the presence of the involved parties, a 'photo matching' was possible for those who could not be physically present. And so, I replied to the Mission Headquarter staff that they should display my photograph: I had complete faith that Reverend Moon would choose the right partner for me.

[6] One of the central tenets of Unificationism is the sanctity of marriage, referred to as 'the Blessing'. Up until recently, marriage partners were suggested for each other by Rev. Moon and this was called 'the matching'; the matching is followed by the official engagement ceremony and then the marriage ceremony.

Heidrun was in Holland leading a fundraising team when she got a call that all sisters twenty-three of age or older should fly to New York to attend the matching. Over 200 members responded to the call. As soon as they arrived at the New Yorker, our international headquarters, they were ushered into the grand ballroom where True Father was already in the process of matching candidates. Heidrun had joined the church in 1977, but she had not yet seen True Father in person. She was overwhelmed and in the process of digesting the whole situation, when True Father asked for the album of photographs of the foreign missionaries who had not been able to attend in person.

Heidrun thinks she had barely been in the room for twenty minutes when suddenly True Father passed by and firmly planted a photo in her hands. My photograph! Following protocol, she left the room to pray about the decision and went up to the reception desk to ask about this 'American boy' (I was a missionary representing America).

Heidrun was perhaps a little perplexed to find out that I was a British missionary in his country of birth. She asked the opinion of the sisters at the desk and was heartened by the nonchalant reply: *"Oh he is a great brother and will accept anyone!"*

And so that was that and our fate was sealed on the 30th of December. Heidrun duly signed the acceptance forms for both of us. A day later, on 31 December 1980, the engagement ceremony was held.

Back in Zambia I was waiting anxiously for news. After a couple of days, a telegram arrived bearing the words: "*You are matched to a German girl and her name is Heidrun and this is her address.*"

I immediately sent a telegram to Heidrun: *"I understand we are engaged; please write first."* Later I was to hear from Heidrun that when she got this communication she thought: "*Well, that is a bossy fellow*!"

Days passed and still no letter arrived. I faithfully trekked down daily to the post office to check our post box, and finally after about a week, there it was – a letter in an unfamiliar handwriting!

That must be it – and so it was with great excitement that I opened the letter. More than anything I was in eager anticipation of finally seeing the face of this 'German girl, Heidrun'. She already knew what I looked like – but why no photo from her? I was disappointed and wrote back in my best diplomatic style: *"Perhaps you could consider including a photo in your next letter."*

At that time, mail between Zambia and Germany took seven days and so it was another two weeks before I received a letter with a very appealing photo. Relief! "*Ah not so bad, a serious person*."

Our first meeting in person was indeed memorable. In January 1982, I was called to attend a conference in New York, and decided to make a stop-over in Frankfurt. (This eventually became the way we could occasionally 'date'; Frankfurt became a stop-over between Zambia and my destination – usually the USA for a conference).

But on this first occasion I really wanted to make a good impression. A night in the cramped economy class of an aircraft is not very conducive to an attractive appearance, and so I decided to shave and freshen up during the refuelling stop in Rome. Disaster! Whether it was tiredness, excitement, or both, I cut myself and was unable to stop the blood from dripping onto my white shirt. Next stop was Frankfurt, and I knew that Heidrun was waiting to see how the real Robert looked compared to his photograph – what would she think? With a pounding heart I proceeded through the entry gate "... *where was she?"*

Just as I was sinking into despair, I heard a voice behind me. *"Robert!"* There she was, the girl from the photograph, Heidrun, beaming all over! Later, she confided that she had been behind a pillar to sneak a look at me first and prepare herself! Well, at least she did not run away!

The Blessing ceremony took place on 1 July 1982, when along with 2,074 other couples we were blessed in eternal matrimony by Rev. and Mrs. Moon in Madison Square Garden, New York. This event attracted huge media coverage; Reverend Moon has explained that one's wedding, the most precious experience, should be witnessed by the whole world!

1 July 1982, our Blessing ceremony, Madison Square Garden, New York, 2,075 couples.

The day before the Blessing, I had a profound experience. As I lay on my bed, I started to weep uncontrollably. It was as if all my ancestors had descended and were celebrating this momentous occasion with me. Adherents of our faith believe that through this Holy Blessing, not only does the participating couple receive personal redemption from sin, but that the whole lineage is involved. I continued to sob for nearly an hour as I understood that our marriage is no ordinary marriage, but involves the past, present and future.

1 July 1982, our Blessing (wedding), New York.

We have been blessed with five children, born in almost as many countries. Our first two daughters were born in the same hospital as I was, Luanshya Mine hospital in Zambia, and our sons in Zimbabwe, Germany, and Scotland. All are now adults and scattered over three continents – America, Australia, and Europe – as are our five grandchildren. Our church stresses "true love, true life and true lineage" and the leaving of a legacy of descendants who "live for the sake of others".

The couples in our church – at least in those days – often started off as strangers and even 'enemies'. Sometimes great effort was needed to overcome racial, cultural, and individual differences and outlooks, but the reward for perseverance has been in most cases a lasting, truly romantic love. As we change and come to know more and more deeply the heart of the other, we come to see the love of God that binds us together. Even now, the rate of divorce in our movement remains exceptionally low as each couple strives to become an ideal eternal couple.

Chapter Six:
Zambia: Our Activities Expand

The vision of our Founders extends beyond simply establishing a religious movement: indeed, their hope is to connect all aspects of life to God. As explained earlier (Chapter 4), Rev. Moon emphasised the importance of a strong financial foundation with businesses run in a principled way. He also stressed involvement in, for example arts, culture, and academic life and his vision was that we missionaries develop such a tradition in our countries.

New York 1982, Reverend Moon personally signing a book for me.

PWPA (Professors World Peace Academy) was founded in 1973 by Rev Moon with the goal of promoting and coordinating peace efforts amongst academics and civil servants.

PWPA activity in Zambia began in 1983. Over the course of several visits, we invited many of the professors at the University of Zambia to attend the country's first PWPA conference. However, the Principal of the university, on learning that the conference was connected to Rev. Moon, issued a communiqué, strongly dissuaded all university personnel from cooperating with PWPA in any way. One brave professor, Dr. Gatian Lungu, then the Assistant Dean of Graduate Studies, defied the directive and was the only Zambian professor to attend. Fortunately, the success of the conference was secured by the attendance of eleven professors from other African countries.

In 1984 Dr. Lungu became the president of Zambia PWPA, and the organization was formally registered with the Zambian government. Dr. Lungu took over the responsibility of inviting other professors and in 1984 the Zambian participation rose dramatically to twelve, with another twelve having to be turned down due to a lack of funding. Along with fifteen other professors from neighbouring countries a final total of twenty-seven high calibre guests attended the conference that year, nine of whom held doctorates earned in the United States or England. The professors shared the broad vision that institutions of higher learning should not be detached from, but rather should truly serve the needs of the people and the nation.

A successful 1985 event was held in Livingstone. Here is an excerpt from PWPA's International Special Report dated April 1986:

"The third conference of PWPA in Zambia convened on June 29 at the Mosi-o-Tunya Intercontinental Hotel in Livingstone, just a few minutes' walk from the world-famous Victoria Falls. Thirteen papers were presented on the theme: 'The University and the Challenge of Youth Development.'"

1989, Leadership of Zambia and the region.

Even though those participating represented a dozen different academic fields, the group was quite cohesive, and the professors were very enthusiastic about having an opportunity to share their views. In the papers presented, African universities were urged to move away from the purely academic, elitist approach to education, to become more community-oriented, and to assist governments in implementing youth development programs in rural areas. We were quite honoured that the district governor sent his deputy to read a speech he had prepared for the conference. This was the first time that a ranking government official had spoken at a PWPA function and his speech was quoted in the Daily Mail, one of the two national newspapers.

The proceedings of these conferences were published and even today references to the original publications are made in academic books. Indeed, the 1986 PWPA report continues:

"In 1985 the Zambian PWPA published, with its own resources, the proceedings of the fifth PWPA seminar of the Eastern, Central and Southern African regions. The title of the book is: 'The University and the Challenge of Rural Transformation in the 1980s and Beyond'."

It is our hope that PWPA activities will continue to develop to communicate Rev. Moon's ideals to Zambian academics, who might inspire their students, policy makers, and eventually the entire nation.

Twikatane Medical Clinic was another venture inspired by our Founders' vision.

In 1976 IRFF (International Relief Friendship Foundation) was established to tackle poverty and the unequal distribution of resources, and it was under the auspices of IRFF that a team arrived in the early 1980s to establish a medical clinic to serve Zambia's poorer community. A facility with consulting rooms, waiting rooms, dispensary, staff, and treatment rooms was built in Lusaka West, near the sausage factory. It was staffed by a team of medical professionals from our international community, headed by Dr. Takigawa. The Ministry of Health, although not able to give financial support, greatly appreciated this venture, which also employed some local health professionals.

The clinic, which in its heyday had a daily turnover of more than one-hundred patients, had to be self-supporting; thus, we charged a small fee which was ultimately subsidized by Twikatane Farms sausage factory.

A scar on my left hand is a permanent reminder of my brief experience as a patient after a brush with a drill while carrying out some handiwork. I rushed over to the clinic and, after getting a scolding from sister Eunice, was treated and sent on my way. It has served as a cautious reminder in my subsequent attempts as a handyman!

Unfortunately, when the missionaries left Zambia in 1993, lack of government financial support meant that we ended up having to close the clinic. The premises are still used for accommodation, however, and theoretically the clinic could be revived with the right concept, staff, and finances.

Development of schools.

Missionary work almost inevitably involves schools and education, and this was no different in Zambia.

In August 1984 we purchased a small private secondary school in Chilenje, a township of Lusaka. *Chilenje Independence School* with Mrs. Singh as headmistress was established. Our missionary Steve Buono helped with the administration and taught English. One of the highlights was the visit of President of Zambia, Dr. Kaunda on 24 October 1984, the 20th anniversary of Zambia's independence. It was also his 60th birthday. The school was near to where he had lived during the colonial era, and he enjoyed his visit and greatly encouraged us in our endeavours. The school grew into a facility of over one hundred students, and the government was impressed with our continuous expansion.

This venture inspired us to build our own school and so later in 1984 we started construction of '*Barlastone Park Primary School*' on our fifteen-acre farm in Lusaka West. The school is situated on the outskirts of Lusaka, in one of the poorest districts of the city and the main road is sometimes almost impassable in the rainy season.

Construction progressed slowly with the addition of one classroom per year over a period of fourteen years. It finally became a full primary and secondary school in 1996 and at one time catered for 461 pupils with an average class size of thirty. Basic fees to cover teacher salaries and administration and maintenance expenses are charged, but the school is dependent on donations and sponsorship for development and expansion.

All teachers are fully qualified holders of the Zambian Teachers Certificate and the school offers the final national certificate examination. Pupils who make the grade can enter the University of Zambia and many have gone on to pursue higher education and have become leaders in society.

An encounter many years later, in 2005 in the UK, was an inspiring reminder that any investment can produce an often totally unexpected outcome. I had returned to my hometown in Scotland and was now working as a recruitment consultant. On this occasion I was interviewing a young lady. I asked her home country: '*Zambia*'. And what school did she attend? '*Barlastone Park Primary School*'. No way! I almost fell off my chair. I explained that I was one of the founders of the school and it was her turn to be surprised! I am happy to report that she passed all the interview processes and hopefully is doing well in her career. This was a reminder for me that one of our basic human rights is to receive a basic education and confirms that we have every right to be proud of our educational work in Zambia.

Our financial foundation also continued to expand; between 1985 and 1990, we experienced unprecedented economic growth and our contribution to the employment market attracted much support from the government. We were now one of the nation's best known food manufacturers.

Circa 1990, Fellow missionaries Zambia – left to right Wiesner, Faerber, Yamashita, Williamson, Sasada, Schneider, Fyers.

The developments of one of these projects, Maposa Farm, a cattle ranch, deserves special mention. An abandoned farm near Luanshya in the Copperbelt region in north Zambia became available for purchase opening a whole new opportunity for us. This property consisted of 7,500 acres of land, a ruined farmhouse, a dam, and some broken fences. The area is called 'Maposa', a name given by Chief Malibeka of the Lamba people and means 'throw away'. Geoffrey Fyers arrived from New Zealand to take charge of this project, and with a strong team of Zambian brothers and sisters the farmhouse was completely rebuilt, the area fenced and a stock of cattle obtained – all within five years. Everyone felt strong; after all we were building the Kingdom, not only spiritually, but physically as well and it was a wonderful feeling to see structures going up all over Zambia! At one time we had nearly five hundred sturdy Braham cattle, a breed well-suited to a hot climate and resistant to parasites. I always enjoyed visiting the farm, which was a forty-minute flight from Lusaka.

On visits to the farm in the early days we would sleep in the unfinished house under the stars; looking up at the clear African nights and hearing the swishing of bats flying in and out of the rooms, we did not sleep much!

Today the name '*Twikatane*' – our holding company – is a household name which evokes the knowing response: "*Ah the sausage makers!*" Under its umbrella there were several activities including: the sausage factory, an abattoir, a chain of retail shops, five farms of sizes ranging from a six-acre pig farm to a fifty-acre farm in the Copperbelt, an engineering company, Bretherton Brothers Ltd, Sunshine Commercial Enterprises Ltd, Twikatane Botswana (Pty) Ltd, and Siavonga leisure plot on the shores of Lake Kariba. Later many of the business assets were reorganised and consolidated with the purchase of the 'Peace Embassy' – a prime real estate plot in downtown Lusaka which today is the headquarters of the movement in Zambia.

Twikatane farm, Lusaka, Zambia – Sausage factory production area.

Heidrun joins me

A significant event for me on a personal level, was the arrival of Heidrun in Zambia at the end of 1983. Unlike me she had never lived anywhere other than the 'civilised West' and now she had to deal not only with a new husband but with a totally new environment. Just how different Africa was to Germany was brought forcibly to her attention on one visit to the Maposa farm. Our car became stuck in the sand just inside the perimeter gate and we got out to inspect the damage. Looking for some wood to put in front of the wheels to get the car moving again, Heidrun nearly stood on a huge snake, curled around the bottom of a tree. What a sight! Heidrun's heart stopped beating for a moment before she quietly retreated and told me what she saw. It was a sleeping puff adder, one of the most poisonous snakes in Africa. This species, which also attacks other mammals, is responsible for most of the snakebite fatalities in Africa. Puzzled by our delay, Geoff arrived in the beaten-up land rover and took the lead in killing the snake. Its skin was duly displayed as an ornament and a warning.

Heidrun adapted well to her new life and lent invaluable support to our missionary work. At the same time, she managed the accounts of our three retail outlets. Meanwhile, our family flourished: four of our five children were born during our time in Africa.

I am happy and proud to have played my part in Zambia. Many of the projects were led by our brothers and sisters, and many who came to us originally as employees later became active members of the Unification Community.

Through the projects and businesses, we could demonstrate a spirit of "living for the sake of others" and in this way we were able to encourage wider cooperation within Zambian society. Even today Zambia remains one of the most peaceful nations of Africa.

Reverend and Mrs. Moon have always taught the concept of "a shared culture of interdependence, mutual prosperity and universal values" and this has been the ethos behind the development of the global missionary work.

Our eternal thanks go to them, our True Parents who gave us that crucial initial support in 1978, and to later investments which led to the substantial growth of the Zambian mission.

Chapter Seven:
Missionary in Côte d'Ivoire 1990-1992

At the end of 1990 I received an urgent message. The director of the World Mission Department, Reverend Kwak, requested my immediate presence in Seoul, Korea! With trepidation I boarded the plane and during the long flight to Korea had time to reflect and speculate. Was my 15 years of missionary work in Zambia now to come to an end? I prayed and told God that I would obediently follow any direction Heaven had in store for me. My years of experience had showed me that those who follow directions are often on a more stable life path than those who constantly question them. I arrived in Korea in a state of great excitement and was informed that I was to meet Reverend Kwak for lunch.

I arrived on time, scanned the menu, gave my order to the waiter, and settled into my chair. Rev. Kwak asked for my report. I responded with enthusiasm but was fully aware that this was not the reason I had been asked to travel to the other end of the world! After a long silence – Korean custom is to wait unquestioningly until the elder takes the initiative – Reverend Kwak looked at me and said: "*I want you to go to West Africa, Côte d'Ivoire.*"

He launched into some explanatory details and then asked why I was not eating! In what capacity was I to go there? *"As regional director of West Africa."* And with effect from when? "*Immediately*!"

And that was that. In those days there was no formal selection process or interview for new appointments; it was a simple system of assignment with trust in the assumption that the appointee would do his best for God, True Parents, and all mankind.

I called Heidrun and told her to start packing. Needless to say, she was shocked and surprised. We were used to sudden changes in our organisation when we were single; it was easy to move from one place to another. Now we found out that having a family did not change that; it was just a little more complicated. Our children were still too young to appreciate what was going on, so the whole family pitched in to pack and started to get ready for the next chapter of our journey through life.

Only a few days later, we set off for Abidjan, the French speaking capital of Côte d'Ivoire, and regional headquarters of the Unification Church in West Africa. This was the spring of 1991.

I was immediately struck by the enthusiasm of the young members and their passion for the mission. I came to learn that Côte d'Ivoire had adopted not only the language, but also much of the emotional expression that came from French colonialism, manifest in the great articulation and gesturing in meetings and conversation.

The previous leaders, Mr. and Mrs. Rigney, had established a very solid foundation. There was a strong membership with an attendance of about 250 at Sunday Service, a business foundation with a small chain of four hamburger houses, a ginseng tea distribution, a garage opened by the Japanese missionary, and a newly established primary school.

However, the system of administration was very centralised and micro-managed, and I decided to take a different approach. I gathered all the leaders and gave them the opportunity to choose a business or department for which they would like to take responsibility and ownership. Brothers and sisters stepped forward and chose their area. There were initial teething problems, but step by step the newly appointed leaders learnt to make their own decisions. With a robust reporting system in place, all areas of witnessing and business were soon growing very quickly again.

1991, Leadership of Côte d'Ivoire.

I used to really look forward to the Sunday worship service, the highlight of the week. Everyone would dress up in their 'Sunday best' and with their guests participate in a passionate service. One never knew when the service would end and many times when the evangelizing spirit was strong, the proceedings continued for hours, and the collection box was passed round twice or three times.

I remember the first service in which I participated; when the collection plate came round, I duly put in my offering and gave thanks. Thirty minutes later, the MC announced a second offering for the purchase of a musical instrument. Members danced up to the stage waving their money, very flamboyantly placed it in the box and then with an equally exotic dance returned to their seats. What else could I do but again dig into my wallet to fulfil my obligation? I think that Heaven also dances and rejoices to see this display of passion. Guests often stayed for lectures, attended workshops and some took up church membership.

Shortly after I assumed my responsibilities, we had set the goal of holding a grand rally with 1,000 participants; this was achieved within twelve months and was one of the highlights of my two years in Abidjan.

Rally with one thousand participants. 25 May 1991.

Emmanuel Kouassi, the then church president, described the event and its impact on the nation as follows:

"The convention was an excellent tool to witness openly to the nation about our church and its activities. Our guests included three

national government officials, one Catholic choir, one choir from the National Arts Institute and all the national leaders of our church region – Burkina-Faso, Benin, Togo, and Niger. One thousand people, including our members, gathered at the Hotel Ivoire at 3 p.m. to listen to the speeches. The atmosphere was good. After the opening prayer, we sang the National Anthem of Côte d'Ivoire together with the government representatives.

This convention has contributed to a change in our church's image. For example, when the representative of the Minister of Domestic Affairs was asked to give his address, he confessed that prior to his attendance at the convention he did not have such a good image of the Unification Church. But after his rally experience, he is willing to get to know us better. After our regional director's speech, came closing remarks from a representative of the Ministry of Communication. He said that he was already familiar with our church because of the numerous donations we have given to the nation, for which he is very grateful. He assured us that those who persecute us will certainly decline. It was as if God was speaking through this man.

A big monsei cheer closed our first national convention in Côte d'Ivoire in a heavenly way."

As the regional director, I was required to deliver a speech. I had never spoken before in front of such a large audience and was very weak in French, the official language of the country. It was decided that I would speak in English and Reverend Bakary Camara would be my translator. (Reverend Camara, originally from a Moslem background in Mali, was the very capable leader of our church office.)

It was truly a wonderful occasion and through the rally our church grew very substantially with pioneer activities developing in several towns, such as Bouake.

March 1991, San Pedro, Côte d'Ivoire, Reunited with fellow missionaries from Zambia Randy and Margret Orr.

PWPA.

Côte d'Ivoire held its first PWPA conference on 1 November 1991 in Abidjan, opened by Madam Gogoua Alexise, a member of the Social and Economic Council (a government institution).

Scholars from East and West Africa convened to discuss 'The Crisis in Black Africa'.

Through this and subsequent meetings we were able to meet prominent members of society and lay a foundation for constructive dialogue between the church and leaders of the nation about developing the country. This first conference led to the publication of 'La Crise en Afrique Noire', which academic researchers still use as a reference.

Inauguration of Women's Federation for World Peace (WFWP) in Côte d'Ivoire. 15 February 1992.

Côte d'Ivoire was one of the first countries in Africa to open a branch of the WFWP. This has proved to be a wonderful vehicle to reach out to the women in Africa who have historically suffered as having been regarded as no more than property. Programmes have included classes for literacy and sewing, seminars on health and hygiene, and fundraising drives to support local orphanages and schools. The first secretary general was Mrs. Kimbembi Koko, who showed able leadership and pioneered the initial projects with the support of Heidrun and other senior sisters.

Jin-A school

Just as in Zambia, the first missionaries in Côte d'Ivoire established a primary school.

Mrs. Lorette Elias, the school leader had the following to say:

"*Mrs. Kathy Rigney, head of Côte d'Ivoire mission at the time, united the families around this project and helped to launch it. The decision was taken to start with just a preschool and kindergarten in one classroom in the back of their house in 1989.*

The older children started to use a home-schooling program called 'Christian Liberty Academy Satellite Schools' (CLASS).

Mrs. Lorette Elias spent two months in the Jin-A School in New Jersey, USA and on her return decided to enlarge the school project with the help of her husband, Mr. Werner Elias. They united with the vision of UPF Founder, Rev. S. M. Moon, to create a school in West Africa.

In January 1991, the school opened in its current location, found by Mrs. Rigney. We embarked on the project with just one month's rent and the faith that we would rapidly grow. We installed toilets for the young children only and with the authorization of the Ivorian Government opened the school to all. We started with three classrooms and three teachers: Mrs. Sun Sook Houngbedji, Mrs. Petty Kpindy and Mrs. Lorette Elias."

The school has established a strong reputation in Abidjan and Mrs. Lorette Elias is still the headmistress.

Travelling around the region.

As regional director, I was responsible for about ten nations of West Africa, and every few months visited the mission stations to keep updated and to encourage the members. Of all my experiences, there are two which are especially memorable.

On a visit to Niger, our Japanese missionary took us to visit an oasis on the edge of the Sahara Desert. After about a two-hour drive from the capital, Niamey, in a rickety Land Rover along a gravel road, we arrived at our destination. It consisted of some grass and a water outlet, but the main attraction was the remains of one tree. A few years previously, the tree had been knocked over and destroyed by a car reversing into it. I found it extraordinary that such a thing could happen in this very oasis in the whole of the vast emptiness of the desert. What a vivid memory and a great story for the tourists!

December 1992, Sunday Service, with our local leader Kouakou Seraphin, Abidjan.

The second notable experience was of flying into Monrovia, the capital of Liberia. Randy Orr was our missionary to Liberia and responsible for our logging business there, but he was based in Abidjan. One day he asked me to accompany him on a visit to the office in Monrovia. But there was one small problem: there was a civil war raging in the country. How were we to get there? Travelling was hazardous.

We chartered a small single-engine plane and set off from Abidjan in the morning. Tropical storms are quite common in West Africa, and every time we reached a large cumulus cloud the pilot flew around or under it. That was bad enough, but on our approach to Monrovia, the pilot started twisting and turning the plane. It was worse than a roller coaster ride, and I broke out in a cold sweat. After we had safely landed on the pot-holed runway, I dared to ask the pilot why he had manoeuvred the plane in that fashion. His nonchalant reply: "*We might have been mistaken by the rebels for an enemy plane and shot down!*"

Did we really dare fly back to Abidjan that evening after finishing our business? Yes, indeed! When I look back on this episode, I am reminded that when we are doing God's will and fulfilling a public purpose, He is always our protector. I continue to carry a picture of our Founders in my wallet as a reminder of my mission and responsibility as their representative.

The call to Alaska. 20-29 October 1992.

At the end of 1992, all missionaries were called by our Founders to attend an international missionary conference in Kodiak Island, Alaska. But this turned out to also be a fishing training retreat; we received direct guidance from Rev. Moon about how to cast and bait and were sent out in teams of between five and seven onto the cold Pacific Ocean in our

'Good Go' fishing boats. We were also given spiritual guidance that extended into the 'wee hours' of the following day. But my intuition told me that there was perhaps another reason that True Father had gathered the missionaries from all over the world – and sure enough, on the last night of the workshop our Founder in his concluding remarks made a dramatic announcement. "*All Western missionaries are to be reassigned to Russia to help support the new pioneering mission work in that nation after the disintegration of the Soviet Union!*" We looked at each other in amazement. I thought to myself: *"This is going to be dramatic, from the heat of Africa to the depths of winter in Russia!"*

The long flight back to Abidjan gave me ample time for reflection: *"How would I prepare myself for this new mission that God was entrusting to us?"*

October 1992, Holy Day celebration with our Founder in Alaska, USA (front row second from left).

October 1992, Alaska fishing during the workshop with our Founder.

Chapter Eight: Missionary to Russia 1993 -1994

The change of mission in December 1992 from the African heat of Abidjan to a wintry Moscow demanded flexibility and adaptation.

The rest of the family remained in Côte d'Ivoire; the plan was that I would first make a foundation and then they would join me later.

My first impression of Moscow was of a city that was very cold – not only physically, but also spiritually. The buildings were stark and expressionless, and the officials at the airport simply glowered at me as they checked my passport.

It must be borne in mind that the Soviet Union had just been dismantled the previous year and Boris Yeltsin was in his first year as president of the new Russia. The country was still in chaos and the rouble-dollar rate extremely unstable. For the first few months I kept both currencies in my pockets, trying to keep abreast of the rapidly – up to three times daily – changing rate.

All the new arrivals were invited to participate in an orientation seminar, after which we were to receive our assignments. This seminar was held in a Moscow hotel, and was headed up by the continental leader, Dr. Seuk.

We were over one hundred in number – missionaries from all over the world who were used to facing all kinds of challenges, including adapting to local diets quite different from our own. Now we were being introduced to the staple Russian fare: an endless buffet of the famous 'borscht' (a sour soup made from beetroot), sturgeon caviar (a cheap tinned version from the Caspian Sea), Russian fatty sausage, mounds of bread, tea served with heaps of sugar and the occasional cake with icing. The first and maybe second meal was a novelty, but the same cuisine every meal and every day was very unappetising and tedious. How I longed for a bowl of cornflakes or a fresh croissant and filter coffee!

Having survived the menu, the next challenge was to 'survive' the nights. We were informed that we Westerners were seen by all the girls as a potential ticket out of Russia, and to expect calls at night. Sure enough, the phone would ring and on the other end of the line a heavy-breathing female voice would ask in English: "*Do you need some company?*" The girls enticed the reception staff with a small payment to provide the room numbers of Western gentlemen. I quickly learnt my first Russian word '*nyet'– no!* and had to use it often!

At the end of the seminar, we were all assigned to a mission area, and set off in small groups from Moscow Central Station. Some were embarking on a journey of three or more days to the outer reaches of Siberia.

My destination was the just over twenty hours distant Rostov-on-Don. I had been appointed as regional leader to south-west Russia, centred on this town.

I travelled with Werner Elias, the original German missionary to Côte d'Ivoire, who had been assigned to Krasnodar. The train was a massive metal beast, typical of Soviet Russia. We had a little compartment to ourselves and our first task was to befriend the larger than life "babushka", the carriage hostess. A couple of dollars ensured that we were well taken care of and kept amply supplied with sweetened tea, sausage, cheese, and bread. Our journey was made! We travelled day and night, with stops at many towns and villages to pick up passengers. But everything seemed so bleak and cold and the people very disgruntled. The population was quickly waking up to the fact that they had been cheated by the communist system for the previous seventy years and were finding out that Russia was not the utopia on earth but was far behind the West.

Our Moscow headquarters had informed us that we would be met by Russian student graduates who were to be our translators. Sure enough, I was greeted at the station by Natasha. She spoke perfect English and took us to our accommodation, a small apartment owned by some Armenians. In the building there were also two classrooms and an upstairs room with a piano.

Werner continued his journey to his town and Natasha and I were left in Rostov-on-Don. I registered with the British Embassy and was somewhat taken aback to be informed that I was the only British citizen in the city of nearly one million. I made sure to write the Embassy's telephone number down in my diary!

I was treated a bit like a celebrity and received many invitations for endless rounds of Russian tea and cake. The town had been cut off from the outside world for seventy years and the residents, thrilled to meet a British person for the first time in 'the flesh', were anxious to introduce themselves. I moved mostly in academic circles, giving lectures on the "Divine Principle" in schools, colleges, and the university. I was not quite sure as to what motivated the participants to attend. Was it to practice their English and see an English lecturer? Or were they interested in spiritual matters? No matter what, it was wonderful to lecture and the audiences were usually thirsty for knowledge. Russia has a long history of spirituality expressed in the Russian Orthodox Church and many people were eager for a new spiritual message to fill the void left by oppression. Natasha was a brilliant translator, had studied our teaching methodically and was able to answer questions, adding her own insights.

Anapa

In January 1993 we were called to Anapa on the Black Sea for a three-day workshop for academics. Over five-hundred participants from south-west Russia as well as a delegation from Armenia were in attendance. The accommodation was in a Soviet era spa resort, with huge stark murals, cold marble, and austere furniture. Although the lectures were held in a bleak auditorium, the atmosphere was electric as hundreds gathered to hear the word of God from a group of Westerners. Our translators did a wonderful job and in the evening each region entertained us by performing traditional dances. I could not understand the Russian language or dialects, but strongly felt God being expressed in the culture. I reflected that even though His word could not be spoken out under communism, God was still present in the broken hearts of the people and could be expressed in the song and dance. Many tears were shed as we heard testimonies of mistreatment during the Soviet era and of how individualism and creativity were crushed by the State, leaving the people in a stupor.

Winter is harsh in Russia and it was not easy to keep warm during the workshop, even with layers of coats. I discovered that a long soak in a deep bath with hot water allowed the heat to penetrate my bones and keep me going for several days.

Maybe the harsh winters are yet another reason why those tall, blond, blue-eyed girls longed to leave the country. We were still seen as an 'exit visa' and I gave Natasha strict instructions to keep these girls at bay. Whatever she said had a highly effective and dramatic effect. I wish I had been able to understand the Russian language!

Rostov-on-Don: English language school

On our return to Rostov-on-Don after the workshop, I suggested to the others that we establish an English language school. Thus, the first private English school in the city was opened. As soon as it became known that it was run by a native English speaker, we were in great demand. We offered two or three classes daily, using textbooks that I had brought over from the UK. It was also a fertile witnessing initiative and several students attended our faith lectures. This resulted later in exchange visits to Scotland which cemented the membership even more.

As regional leader, I also had to visit neighbouring towns such as Volgograd, Krasnodar, and Pyatigorsk. Pyatigorsk is famous as the KGB university town of languages – specialising in English, German, and Spanish. And what an eerie town! It felt like everyone was suspiciously watching each other.

Left: Circa 1993 Rostov-on-Don, Russia with fellow missionary Elias and our Russian translator Natasha. Right: Circa 1993 our Russian language school brochure.

My trip there remains one of my most vivid and terrifying memories. I made the journey in a twin- engine propeller plane run by the state airline, Aeroflot. I was crammed in the back with five other passengers, boxes of live chickens and a couple of fifty-gallon drums of diesel fuel. Health and safety in those days were not a priority; it was more of a question of getting from A to B! Fortunately, it was a short flight, and I could fulfil my purpose of visiting our pioneer missionary.

Circa 1993, with students at our English language school in Rostov-on-Don, Russia.

Health scare

Whether it was due to too much Russian tea and sugary cake, or to the stress of being alone in Rostov-on-Don as the only foreigner I do not know; but one day my heart protested and shifted into an overactive rhythm. This was very scary, and I decided that I should return to Scotland for medical tests, which fortunately ruled out heart disease. However, at about the same time we received direction from

Moscow that if our families were unable to join us, we should return to our home countries. My request to Rev Kwak, the International Mission Department director, for permission to relocate back to Scotland and carry out 'home church'[7] work, was granted. I travelled back to Abidjan and together with Heidrun and the children we arrived back in Scotland and so began our next chapter in Edinburgh. To this day I am grateful to the Côte d'Ivoire church mission, who sent us some support money for a few months while we settled in Scotland.

---

[7] Neighbourhood outreach

Chapter Nine:
Back to Edinburgh

My return in 1994 to Edinburgh marked the completion of a full circle. This was where my spiritual journey had begun twenty-two years previously.

Edinburgh – 'Auld Reekie'– the capital of Scotland, had not changed so much, but I certainly had. And I was no longer a single missionary, but a married man with a family of four children – and a fifth on the way – to support. One of our children would be born in Scotland! What was God expecting me to do now? As a family we embarked on this new chapter with much prayer and devotion as we sought to find out how we could earn a living while continuing to live a public life of faith. My CV was not one that was likely to inspire any conventional prospective employers and I felt that I had two career options; either to become a door-to-door insurance salesman or to start my own business. Was I an idealistic dreamer? Maybe, but the dream of opening my own coffee house would not leave me. The plan was acceptable to our relatives to the extent that I was given the necessary financial support.

'Williamson's Bakehouse' was established.

Perhaps my closing remarks in an interview for our church magazine in 1995[8] convey the essence of my attitude:

---

[8] *Today's World*

"I think that it is vital to live a public life. We have to be seen in society doing things in society. If one becomes centred on oneself, it is very difficult for God to work through us in the community. We need to have public positions and live publicly, and then God can work."

Circa 1994, meeting former President Kaunda of Zambia in London.

December 2003, meeting President Arafat during the Middle East Peace Initiative tour

Williamson's Bakehouse.

For the three years from 1994-1997, this was our life, and it was tough! Profit margins were narrow, and money just seemed to move from one pocket to the other. The character of the neighbourhood, predominantly a student area, continually changed and we evolved accordingly. We started off purely as a bakery, and even employed a baker from Germany to teach us how to make special German bread; then we became a coffee shop; and finally developed into the 'Zambezi Restaurant' with a menu of exotic African dishes. Unusual meats imported from South Africa via London were delivered to our restaurant the following day. This caused quite a stir amongst the city council Health and Food Standards Committee and I well remember the day when two young officials arrived in my kitchen and asked to inspect the crocodile tail meat. A horrified expression crept over their faces when I unhesitatingly set off in the direction of the storeroom to oblige! But when I arrived back in the kitchen with a couple of vacuum-packed crocodile portions, their horror was dissipated, and they burst out laughing. They surely thought I had gone off to get a whole crocodile carcass! We passed the inspection with flying colours and were not bothered further.

Many customers were attracted by the unusual cuisine in a restaurant run by someone who had been born in and had first-hand knowledge of Zambia. I loved working 'out front' with our clients and supplying them with background information on the dishes.

"There was an Irish chef working in an African restaurant in Scotland" sounds like the beginning of a bad joke, but we did

actually have one! I had a lot of fun working with our Irish chef, Mark, who concocted beautiful sauces. We even attracted the attention of the National BBC Good Food Guide and were invited for a telephone interview. But alas, the profit margins proved just too narrow and when someone presented us with a cheque for the business, we decided to accept it and move on.

1995, Williamson's Bakehouse, Edinburgh.

Call from London.

Towards the end of 1997 I got a call from London from President Young Whi Kim, the Korean elder who was supervising the movement in the UK at that time. *"Robert, I would like you to be the community leader of Scotland."*

I had not held a public church mission for three years, and while I was quite happy to support my local pastor as an older brother, I was unsure about assuming leadership. Was God calling me again to the front line? I expressed my uncertainty to President Kim, but the Korean character does not willingly accept anything less than clarity and conviction and he refused to put the phone down until I agreed. What else could I do? Thus, a new challenge was presented to me and my family. Our church membership in Scotland was small, consisting of about twenty families scattered over different parts of the nation, but we were optimistic about growth. We owned two properties; I managed to sell one and invested the proceeds to increase the portfolio to three. One of these properties was a shop on Easter Road, a main thoroughfare in a working-class area of Edinburgh, which we refurbished and opened as a 'storefront' church. This property served as an office and internet cafe during the week and a venue for the congregation of between thirty and thirty-five who gathered for worship on Sundays.

I encouraged everyone to go 'back to basics' and to witness (evangelise) on the streets and distribute pamphlets inviting people to the worship service. Rev. Moon had changed the name of our church – in keeping with the desire to work together with people of all faiths - and we were now known as the 'Family Federation for World Peace and Unification' (FFWPU)[9]; it was truly a wonderful day when we

---

[2] The Family Federation for World Peace and Unification was established in 1994 by Reverend Sun Myung Moon. Reverend Moon stated at the founding of the FFWPU that he never intended to create a new religion, but to open an age after religion where families would serve

were able to display our sign in Edinburgh for the whole nation to see.

I have fond memories of that time of grassroots activity. One day, when I was walking down Easter Road distributing church pamphlets to all the shop owners, I entered a shop selling African food. I was greeted by a very energetic African lady and noticed straight away that she was reading the Bible. I expressed to her my surprise and delight to have found one person in the whole street who was reading the Holy Scriptures, and this remark led to a deeper conversation. Following our meeting, Roseline started to attend our services and retreats and remains an active supporter of all our interfaith work. She has spoken at our events, encouraging everyone to listen to the Unificationist message.

During this time, we held frequent interfaith retreats and one-day seminars in Edinburgh. These were attended by guests from all religious faiths, sharing the same platform. A comment frequently voiced was: "*Only the Unificationists can bring everyone together.*" I felt our role was to express the heart of God, our Heavenly Parent and that God expresses Himself through all faiths. It is up to us to overcome our prejudices and unite harmoniously together as brothers and sisters. Many who have contributed to these seminars have continued to support us and some have gone on to receive the Holy Blessing of marriage. This Blessing, under the banner of FFWPU, proclaims the global aspect of God's heart

---

as the core of spiritual and character growth. [Previously, what was known as the 'Unification Church' had been established (in Korea in 1954) as the Holy Spirit Association for the Unification of World Christianity.]

by bringing couples together in the sanctity of marriage and strengthening the foundation of life which is the family.

Dr. Hak Jan Moon's visit to Scotland

The highlight of my time as Scottish community leader was the visit of Dr. Hak Ja Han Moon, True Mother – now also affectionately known as the 'Mother of Peace' – to Edinburgh on 21 May 2000 as part of one of her world tours. I was there with the security team at Edinburgh Airport to await the arrival of her private jet. Our small convoy escorted her to the Balmoral Hotel, one of the most prestigious hotels in Scotland, which boasts a superb location on Princes Street, overlooking the Castle. True Mother had stayed in this hotel on her previous visit to Scotland in 1991 and remembered straight away: "*Oh, I know this hotel.*"

The courteous hotel staff provided her entourage with a whole wing consisting of a private kitchen, dining area and bedroom suite.

The official programme was scheduled to begin that very afternoon, and the grand ballroom filled up to capacity with those who were eager to hear the spiritual message directly from this distinguished leader from the Orient. True Mother gave a beautiful address with a rousing call to action, "*that we all join in working to build God's heavenly kingdom on earth,*" which was enthusiastically received and thunderously applauded by the interfaith audience. Her address was followed by a presentation of service awards to several prominent Scottish VIPs.

After the event we members were invited by True Mother to meet in a small room for a 'victory celebration', the highlight of which was a telephone call between True Mother and True Father, who had been following the speech on live streaming in the United States. The atmosphere was beautiful and electric and we all really felt that we were in heaven. Our ten-year-old second son, much to the chagrin of the security team, jumped up and hugged True Mother as she was leaving the room, causing her to beam brightly. Stephan surely has a memory to cherish for a lifetime!

21 May 2000, True Mother's speech in Scotland (Edinburgh castle esplanade).

I do not know if True Mother directly commented about the Scottish welcome of full-dress kilts and bagpipes, but she must have been impressed because on the way back to the airport she requested to visit Edinburgh Castle. Our convoy swung up the 'Mound' to the site first established in the Iron Age as a hill fort and built as a castle for King David in 1103. I presented a brief history of Edinburgh as we stood on the esplanade overlooking the city. This moment in time was captured in another photograph which is part of the historic collection in my Scottish office.

Jardim, Brazil 2000

The year 2000 was marked by two events of personal significance.

In that year, I graduated from the Open University (distance learning facility) with a degree in Social Sciences. Having abandoned my education as a teenager, I felt it no mean achievement to obtain a degree as a (very) mature student of almost fifty years of age!

December 2000, Glasgow. Open University graduation as a mature student with Heidrun, my mother and stepfather Ralph.

And the second event was significant for our whole family. We were one of many Unificationist families who responded to Rev. and Mrs. Moon's open invitation to participate in one of the forty-day 'Ideal Family' workshops which were ongoing in Jardim, Brazil. These workshops were designed to give attending families a taste of 'ideal family life'.

The prospect of a forty-day workshop with a young family was daunting enough – but first we had to get there. The journey itself was an expedition: taking a family of two adults and five children between the ages of fourteen and six all the way to South America. The memory of the seven Williamson family members occupying the whole row of the Boeing 747 remains vividly etched in my mind. Heidrun and I anticipated the journey ahead with some trepidation, but the children were simply excited. The long flight to Sao Paulo via London was only the first leg of our expedition; an overnight bus ride of over one thousand kilometres to our final destination, Jardim in the State of Mato Grosso do Sul, still lay before us.

And so, about two days after leaving Edinburgh, the Williamson family arrived in Jardim, Brazil, and immediately launched into the forty-day seminar at the New Hope Farm. The climate was perfect and the natural environment unbelievable; it is really a Garden of Eden. The mornings were devoted to lectures, prayer and meditation; and the afternoons to diverse activities such as fishing from the banks of the river, horse riding for the kids and local field trips. Our Founders really encouraged us to explore nature and to take every opportunity to interact with our surroundings on the various fishing boat trips. In the evenings, the international flavour of our Unification community was reflected in the cultural presentations of song and dance and in the testimonies where people shared life stories and special moments. Families from all over the globe participated in these workshops.

We had numerous interesting experiences, and very quickly learned two important points which were essential for our well-being:
– any snacks could survive the onslaught of ants and insects in our room when hung on a piece of string tied between the bunk beds and:
– before sitting on the toilet, it was advisable to check that there were no frogs in hiding. Neglect of this precaution might cause one to sustain an almighty shock!

We were honoured to have a visit from Rev. and Mrs. Moon during the seminar. A photograph of our family together with them now has pride of place on the wall in my office at home in Scotland. After forty days, we embarked on the long journey back to Scotland, which luckily was smooth and uneventful.

This was no 'budget holiday.' It took us a year to pay off the credit card expenses. But it was of enormous value to our family, and I personally could meet God again in those peaceful surroundings and had many deep realisations. It was strongly affirmed to me that our life should really be one of service to others so as to help those less fortunate in this world.

Chapter Ten: Regional Director of the Balkans, 2006-2013

Our family settled into life in Scotland. I became a self-employed consultant in 1999 with 'Blue Arrow Personnel Services' as my agent. My contracts varied in length from a few days to weeks or months and my task was to conduct competency-based interviews involving checking keyboard skills and phonetic alphabet as well as role-play exercises. I also studied for and obtained my professional HR qualifications, which enabled me to become a member of the British Psychological Society and to conduct psychometric testing. This opened the door to work for the Scottish government as a recruiter for the Crown Office and Registers of Scotland in addition to telephone interviewing for the secret service MI5 – all of which boosted the pay-check! Meanwhile my family were all attending High School or University.

Then, at the beginning of 2006, I was asked by President Song, the spiritual head of our church in Europe, to assume the position of Regional Director of the Balkans. This region, consisting of Albania, Macedonia, Kosovo, Bulgaria, and Greece was – especially at that time – a very troubled area where strongly held Christian and Moslem beliefs clashed. It had been a battleground until 2001, only five years before my appointment.

I was able to hand over my responsibility as Scottish pastor to Paul Currie and could continue my consulting work, juggling work assignments with visits to the Balkans, which were rarely longer than one week.

My primary task in this region was to facilitate and encourage reconciliation. I was to accompany President Song on his visits and to reach out to a broad spectrum of society – in particular, to develop our work with youth and to introduce the Universal Peace Federation (UPF)[10] at the highest levels of government and leadership. In addition to private meetings, this involved workshops for young people and regional seminars introducing UPF's programmes.

In some of the Balkan countries, an already strong foundation greatly facilitated our work. For example, Mrs. Moon had already visited Albania three times; alone in May 2000, with her husband Dr. Moon in October 2005, and with one of her sons, Kook Jin in July 2006. In 2005, Dr. and Mrs. Moon had met the then President of Albania, Alfred Moisiu, and in the following year Mrs. Moon had delivered a speech entitled "God's Ideal Family and the Kingdom of the Peaceful, Ideal World" to leading figures in the government and society. It is no coincidence that the work of UPF has flourished in Albania, which now has local peace councils in each

---

[10] Founded in 2005 by Rev. Dr. Sun Myung Moon and Dr. Hak Ja Han Moon, UPF is a global network of individuals and organizations dedicated to building a world of peace in which everyone can live in freedom, harmony, cooperation and prosperity. UPF is an NGO in general consultative status with the Economic and Social Council of the United Nations.

of the nation's sixty-one municipalities and is active on all levels in many fields.

Experiences in Kosovo

Kosovo suffered greatly in the Balkan wars and is often dismissed as a part of 'greater Albania' because of its Moslem and Albanian majorities. The country is still not a member of the UN and Russia refuses to recognise its 2008 declaration of independence from Serbia, an ally of Moscow. Once more, religious differences between Orthodox Christians in Serbia and Moslems in Kosovo are at the root of the dispute. Both sides lay claim to territory where they have sacred sites.

Of course, such disputes are not limited to the Balkans. Sadly, our world is littered with them. Yet again and again I find myself asking: why can mankind not emphasize spirituality rather than religious dogma? On one visit to Kosovo, I experienced something which illustrates this well. One of my Moslem friends from the UK and I were invited out to dinner and were presented with the traditional drink of 'cherry plum raki'. My Moslem friend politely declined, commenting that as a Moslem he did not drink alcohol. To this our hosts declared that they too were Moslem but that as this was a traditional drink it was quite acceptable! Then followed a heated exchange with much bandying of quotes from the Qur'an to justify what a 'proper' Moslem was. I quietly sipped my orange juice and left it to them to thrash out the dogma. Luckily, the delicious traditional food saved the evening!

A visit to the Balkans leaves one with many pleasant impressions. But experiences on the road are entirely different - the drivers are crazy! One night-time drive through the mountainous escarpment between Kosovo and Albania remains a vivid memory which causes me still to shudder. We had a deadline to meet and our chauffeur, clearly relishing the challenge, set off at high speed.

It appeared that after passing his test (if he ever did!), he threw the rulebook to the wind. His driving style was adventurous. I was glad to be in the back seat and to be protected from a realisation of the full extent of the precariousness of the journey. More than once massive boulders signalled roadworks and forced us to swerve to the right towards the escarpment, where there were only flimsy crash barriers between us and the deep valleys far below. Surely God protected us, as on many other occasions!

But to be fair to drivers in the Balkans, some of those occasions are self-made. I remember once as a young man being asked to drive from Edinburgh to Reading. Instead of waiting for dawn, I set off in the 'wee hours' accompanied by a brother in the passenger seat. Just south of Newcastle it happened. The mishap and the miracle. I must have dozed off and drifted across three lanes on the motorway, only to be abruptly wakened by the grinding of stones on the verge. I slammed on the brakes. We both were shaking and trembling with shock and could only offer a thankful prayer. To this very day, I pray before driving and enforce rigidly the rule that the front seat passenger does not sleep!

Dealing with state security – Bulgaria

Even before my official appointment as regional director, I was asked to accompany and lead a delegation of Scottish church members to Bulgaria. Our task was to assist the local members in their preparations for a visit by Rev. Moon, who was to deliver a speech in the capital, Sofia as part of a 2005 world tour to inaugurate UPF chapters in each nation. The speech was scheduled for 27 October. We had made good progress, had booked the venue, and arranged dignitaries, entertainment, and security. However, unknown to us we were being closely monitored by the Bulgarian secret service. Four days before the event, we were contacted by government officials connected to the Home Office and Internal Affairs who demanded an explanation of our activities. On 26 October, I received a call from Radomir (the church National Leader), informing me that two officials were in our office at the Peace Embassy requesting my immediate presence. I had never dealt with state security before, but naively thought they would clarify the situation. I was greeted by a very worried staff in our embassy and ushered into the main office, where Radomir was waiting with two impeccably dressed gentlemen. After the customary greetings, I asked: "*Did they view the impending arrival the following morning of Rev. Moon as problematic?*" The answer from the official was direct: they were unable to guarantee his safety. "*Did this mean he was banned from entering the country?*" No, but his safety could not be guaranteed. Further details were not forthcoming and when they left, I was in a quandary. How should I advise European headquarters? I could do no other than to report that it would be too risky and dangerous to proceed as planned.

Thus, Rev. Song, as European leader, represented Rev. Moon and delivered the speech. Once again, I realised that we are in a constant battle between the forces of good and evil and that as God works to restore the world, we need to work carefully and prayerfully. Decision making is often difficult, but personal experience has confirmed to me numerous times that prayer is an invaluable help.

December 2010, lecturing at Sofia University, Bulgaria.

Memorable workshop in Corfu, 23-27 September 2010.

Of all the seminars and workshops organised during these years in the Balkans, one of the most memorable was held in the village of Nissaki on Corfu in September 2010. The old people told us that Nissaki – 'little island' in Greek – used to be a small rocky island, which eventually became joined with the mainland. Our group was made up of sixteen participants from Greece, Bulgaria, Macedonia, and Albania. We followed a schedule of 5.00 am morning prayer and meditation, a lecture before breakfast and a further two lectures before lunch. The afternoons were devoted to leisure activities such as swimming or exploring the island. Dinner at 6.00 pm was followed by another lecture before we retired for the night at about 10.00 pm. The temperature of the beautiful aquamarine sea was perfect for swimming, and the olive groves and rugged coastline a delight to the eye. We enjoyed a healthy and abundant Mediterranean diet.

Circa 2010, Regional workshop Corfu, Greece.

The physical beauty and nourishment were complemented by the profound connection the participants made with the spiritual content of the lectures. As the main lecturer I could deeply sense this. Here too, I felt this was like the original 'Garden of Eden'. The seminar passed much too quickly!

Meeting Presidents

This period in the Balkans was also a time when I was able to meet directly with the heads of state of several nations, especially the emerging nations of Kosovo and Macedonia. On our part, we could introduce to them the work of UPF, which had effectively gathered under one umbrella decades of work in a variety of fields. On their part, the leaders of these nations were eager to meet anyone who could facilitate international recognition of their countries. They realised that this was one of the strengths of UPF with its network of international connections. Our delegations were always warmly welcomed and many of these contacts have become staunch supporters of UPF. Initially, I was in awe of the trappings of power with the formal meetings, obligatory photos, cups of coffee, exchange of gifts and protocol documents. But I eventually came to the realisation that at the end of the day, they too are just ordinary citizens doing their best to serve their nations and community. I really admire and respect all those who hold public office; their sacrifice is truly commendable, and they need our prayers and support for their endeavours to serve their nation and – we hope and pray – the wider will of God.

In particular, President Fatmir Sejdiu (Kosovo) went out of his way in 2008 to make us really feel at home in his nation. The Balkans continue to demand our attention and we have ongoing regional conferences to realise a lasting peace in this part of the world.

January 2008, Meeting Fatmir Sejdiu, President of Kosovo with (from left to right) Mrs. Stefanc, Mr. Hyseni, myself, President Song, President Sejdiu, Mrs. Song, Mr. Miller and Mr. Ibraj.

During the years of my mission in the Balkans, I continued to support the Scottish church as much as possible. The focus at that time was on developing the Sunday service and Sunday school, as well as local outreach. I was a committee member and often delivered the Sunday sermon, drawing inspiration from my mission work. I feel I was able to energise the Scottish community somewhat and several members contributed to the Balkans mission either financially or by their attendance at seminars.

2011 March, Meeting President Behgjet Pacolli of Kosovo.

Cancer

2011 was to be a very eventful year for me personally and one in which God would powerfully work. I had noticed a lump on my right chest wall, and for about four months dismissed it as insignificant and expected it to eventually disappear. Isn't it just women who get breast cancer? But then my nipple became inverted and I thought I had better have it checked. After a brief examination, my doctor's expression belied his words of reassurance and I was referred to the surgery department of the local hospital. More reassuring words from the surgeon – but why did he have the same worried look on his face? He took a core biopsy and asked me to return on the following day, 14 April, one day before my fifty-ninth birthday. The result explained the worried looks on the faces of my GP and surgeon: I had breast cancer and would require surgery, a full mastectomy.

My eyes welled with tears as we walked out of the hospital. Heidrun knows that I am not strong when dealing with sickness, and as she squeezed my hand, she expressed the wish to have been the one to have received this diagnosis. Illness in one of a couple keenly affects the other.

The date of my scheduled surgery arrived: 4 May. I was scared. After all the preliminaries, I took my leave of Heidrun and was wheeled by the porter along the corridor to the operating suite. A smile from one of the nurses, a small injection… and that was it. I was gone!

A couple of hours later I woke up on the ward with the right side of my body bandaged up and Heidrun at the bedside. But these two hours of my life - where had they gone and what had happened? I had disappeared; there were no dreams, no visions, nothing. Two hours gone, never to be regained. The two other operations in my life provoked the same experience and reflections.

During the three days in hospital I experienced many emotions; I talked a lot to God and was so grateful for another chance to do something with and give meaning to my life. We are here for such a short time. I determined to continue to help others and set them on their own spiritual journey. The surgeon was Moslem, and I was encouraged and comforted to have a person of faith performing the operation. I felt he could understand my worries and my heart.

The follow up appointments showed that all was well, that chemotherapy and radiation were not necessary, but that I had to take a medication for the next five years.

I passionately believe that much illness has a spiritual cause – the body becomes unsynchronised and needs to be realigned. I had dutifully performed all that had been offered by 'external' /conventional medicine and then decided to focus on the 'internal' spiritual side of the healing process. I attended a twenty-one-day course at our Korean Hyojeong Heaven and Earth Cheonbo training centre in October 2011. This involved daily 5:00 am prayer/meditation and two sessions of chanyang, where different parts of the body are systematically 'slapped' to the rhythm of a big drum and song. The intention is to remove 'evil spirits' and to restore the yin and yang harmony to the body and thus a good body-mind unity.

I am pleased to say that I have had no disease recurrence.

Chapter Eleven:
Africa Calls Again

Although it had now been many years since my mission in Africa, that great continent and especially Zambia, was never far from my thoughts. A very energetic and resourceful young Moslem, Aftikhar Ahmed ('Iffy'), had become connected with our movement in Scotland as an 'Ambassador for Peace'[11] and together we organised from 2011-2013 annual 'fact-finding' tours to Zambia with the goal of engendering interest and financial support for diverse projects. However, it became clear that this strategy alone was not realistic; we needed a reliable way to raise funds. In 2014 we (Iffy's family, Heidrun and I) decided to create a charitable organisation to which we gave the name 'Sunrise Africa Relief'. The mainstay of the charity was to be a thrift shop.[12] All was going according to plan; Sunrise Africa Relief had received official recognition and registration as a charity and we had rented premises for our shop in the High Street in Dunfermline, the ancient capital of Scotland where we now lived. We opened for business in January 2015.

---

[11] Recognition given by UPF to someone who has contributed to peace-fostering activities.

[12] Thrift shops are to be found in abundance in the United Kingdom and proceeds from the sales of donated goods and clothing are channelled to support a very mixed array of worthy causes from medical research to care of the deprived.

Circa 2015, Sunrise Africa Relief Shop, Dunfermline, Scotland.

March 2019, Presentation of computers in partnership of FFWPU Zambia to Makale government school.

Heidrun and I would share the responsibility of running the shop, assisted by a team of other volunteers. All proceeds, after overheads had been paid, were to serve African projects. Now at least the next three years (term of our lease) were settled. Or were they?

As I have so often experienced in my life, God's plans are different...

I was standing in our newly opened charity shop when suddenly the phone rang. It was Kathy Rigney, one of the original missionaries sent to Africa in 1975, who has dedicated her whole life to the spiritual development of that continent and is considered the 'Great Mama of Africa'. I had not spoken to Kathy for years and to suddenly get a call out of the blue was exciting to say the least. And she had not called simply to enquire after my health: "*Would you like to become a special envoy to South Africa?*"

This was a completely shocking and novel suggestion, yet over forty years of a spiritually orientated life had taught me to heed the call of a higher spiritual authority. Not quite clear what being a 'special envoy' entailed, I gave my unhesitating reply: "*Yes – I would!*"

A telephone interview with our International Headquarters confirmed my appointment for the next five years and it was agreed that I could retain my family base in Scotland. But how to prepare for such a mission? I found out that Headquarters was organising a forty-day workshop for all the African leaders and I felt I should participate. Attendance at a workshop, held at our International Training Centre in Korea, meant following a demanding schedule of early morning prayer and daily hikes to the top of a hill. Many a person younger than me finds this challenging, but even at the age of sixty-three I determined to join the predominantly younger participants in this workshop. I was almost – but not quite – able to complete the entire forty-day workshop. But this was not due to my limitations: I was unable to extend my air ticket.

After a short visit home to reorientate and prepare, I was again on the move – this time to South Africa to embark on my new mission. A banner outside our Peace Embassy in Johannesburg proclaiming “Welcome to South Africa Special Envoy Reverend Williamson” was indeed encouraging. It didn’t take long for me to establish a pattern: a few weeks in South Africa, then home to Scotland for a few weeks to recharge and then back to South Africa.

The church at the time was facing many internal challenges, but we all pulled together and as a team under the leadership of Reverend Kunene and later Reverend Leballo as National Leaders, were able to inspire a revival centring on four locations – Johannesburg, Polokwane in the North, Cape Town in the South and George in the East.

The five years flew by, with my time divided between visiting the local chapters of the church mission, meeting traditional leaders and participating in events. But perhaps the word ‘events’ does not do justice to what we witnessed: these were momentous occasions with the potential to reshape Africa’s future, and I remain eternally grateful for the privilege of having been able to play my part.

Meeting traditional rulers

My most memorable meeting was with Chief Raphahlelo of Limpopo province in the north of South Africa. He and his wife received the Marriage Blessing of our church in January 2016.

I remember the first time I visited their palace, situated on a small hill overlooking the plains of Limpopo province. Our local leader in Polokwane set up the meeting and I received a briefing on the protocols of visiting the Chief. I should prepare a gift and wait to be addressed. I was also informed that the youth would give us a traditional welcome and that I should prepare some monetary donation to give to the young dancers as a token of appreciation, individually as the dances progressed. Having been born in Zambia and having visited various traditional rulers before, I was aware of some of the protocols. I prepared myself by asking for God's guidance and put on my best suit and tie – even though the temperature was almost 30 degrees Celsius!

We were a small convoy of three cars and with great fanfare we drove up towards the Palace and were greeted with a wonderful cascade of song, whistles, and shrieks of excitement. The dances were superb, I was given a warm welcome and could present my gifts. The occasion was marked with a banquet and the initiation of a warm relationship, which has strengthened as the years have passed. Whenever I visit South Africa, I try to visit the Palace to pay my respects and to give some sponsorship to the local clinic and community from our charity Sunrise Africa Relief.

Meeting Prophets and religious leaders

Of the many religious leaders, I met in South Africa, one that has left a very memorable and sincere impression is Imboni (Prophet) Dr. Uzwi Lezwe (The voice of the nation)

Radebe of the Revelation Spiritual Home. He has a following of over two million, not only in Southern Africa but also in developing branches overseas. Their website summarises his fundamental teaching:

"The Revelation Spiritual Home (TRSH) is an African indigenous initiated Home (church), based on African spirituality and structured to restore, thus bringing to the fore the consciousness of the African people back to their African spiritual roots. We pride ourselves of being one of the leading custodians of African spirituality teachings with a view to making African spirituality a way of life."

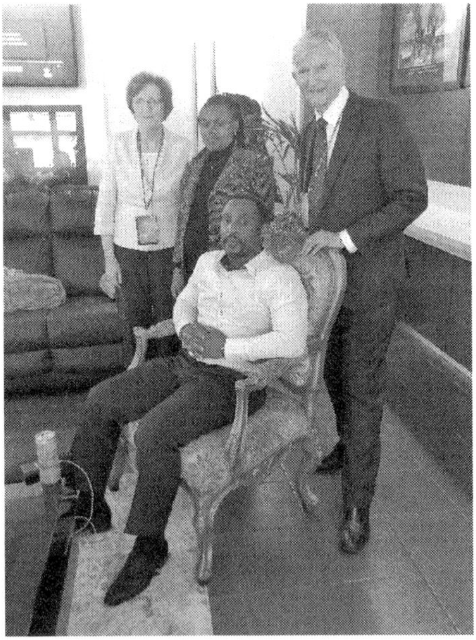

December 2019, Heidrun and I meeting Prophet Radebe and his wife, Johannesburg, South Africa.

I have had the honour of working quite closely with Prophet Radebe over the years. He agreed to become President of the UPF South African branch and subsequently hosted our Founder, Dr. Hak Jan Han Moon at several international joint UPF rallies in South Africa, such as the 'Blessing Festival' on 8 June 2019 at the Orlando stadium in Soweto and the 'Peace Starts with My Family Festival and Continental Marriage Blessing Festival' at FNB stadium in Johannesburg on 7 December 2019, attended by over 50,000 of his followers.

On an earlier occasion I was invited as a representative of UPF to speak at one of his events to launch his association of religious movements 'Inkululeko Yesizwe Association'. I was shown great respect and given a wonderful welcome. The venue was packed with over 10,000 people including government and traditional leaders. As I was waiting to go up to the podium, I sought God's guidance as to what I should say. The previous speakers had all spoken so eloquently, but I prayed: "*What is Your message, Heavenly Parent?*" and then the revelation came. Doubtlessly influenced by my Zambian roots, I danced my way up to the stage! This was met by a roar of approval from the audience and on the podium, I explained that I had received the revelation that God wanted to give Prophet Radebe also another mission, namely, to bring all the races together in South Africa in harmony. The audience roared again and with that I stepped down off the stage and was given a warm embrace by Prophet Radebe!

He repeatedly emphasises that people must go back to their spiritual roots, overcome the constraints of religion and respect one and other.

Africa is exciting in that people are interested in spiritual matters, unlike in the Western world where people feel that their belief is a private matter and that personal matters like religion are not open for discussion.

This became noticeably clear to me once when I was manning a book table in a busy precinct in Johannesburg. Bibles and various books from our church drew quite a positive response and genuine curiosity about our beliefs, but I noticed with interest that while most white South Africans walked past, the black citizens took the time to approach the table. While acknowledging that the history of South Africa is complex, I realise that the white population must relinquish their arrogance and be open to the new South Africa.

Summits across Africa

I had also the privilege of being part of the committee which organised several of the African Summits held by UPF. Each event, starting with the first Africa summit held in Senegal on 18 January 2018 and supported by President Mackie Sall and his government, had its special moments. I was based in Dakar for nearly three months while we coordinated the programme, which involved the government and over fifty nations across Africa, as well as Korea, Europe, the USA, and Japan. There were over 1,000 participants – not only religious, government and traditional rulers, but also representatives from the media and NGOs. The logistics were overwhelming, but with good teamwork and the cooperation of professional agencies, we managed to assemble the programme. Our Founder, Dr. Hak Jan Han Moon was given a welcome to Senegal by President Mackie Sall as befitted a head of state. She was welcomed at the newly built airport by governmental representatives and traditional rulers with dance and song and was then whisked by state security to the hotel and the international conference venue.

2018 November, Mrs. Kathy Rigney and myself present a gift to True Mother, Cape Town, South Africa.

One of the most moving moments of this summit was a special prayer that Mother Moon offered at the House of Slaves on Gorée Island, near the capital city of Dakar. True Mother's tearful prayer surely liberated all the people in Africa who had suffered so much because of the slave trade. In her speech at the World Africa Summit the previous day, she had said, "The continent that I believe has suffered the most is the African continent." She delivered a deep prayer for the ancestors who had endured this painful history, with the belief that there will be a new, heavenly Africa free from

suffering. She then announced the donation of a boat – the *Victoria* – to the island, to transport island patients needing urgent care to the hospital on the mainland of Senegal.
It was also my honour along with Patrick from France to be involved in resourcing and remodelling the boat to fit the purpose of being a boat 'ambulance'.

Patrick wrote the following about the ceremony at which the boat was 'blessed' and handed over to the mayor: *"The last stop was for the blessing of the boat. I had asked the pilot to bring the Victoria as close as possible to the pier. Holding a bowl of Holy Salt, True Mother, with two daughters-in-law, Julia HJ Moon and Yeon Ah Moon, and assisted by the mayor and me, went as near as possible to the boat. We laughed just a bit when the Holy Salt did not reach the boat because it was moving in the wind. I offered to take part in the ceremony and even said to Mayor Senghor, 'You could also bless your boat.' Mother looked on, smiling, as we both took a handful of Holy Salt and threw it. This time it went on the boat – a victory for Victoria!"*

I also had an opportunity to visit many of the religious leaders of the country – various brotherhoods or Sufi movements [like religious orders, or distinct spiritual paths] - such as the Murid, the Tijaniyya and others. I was invited one evening by Sheikh Mansour Diouf, the leader of the Murid Brotherhood in Senegal and chair of the organising committee for the African Summit, to a religious meeting in a suburb of Dakar. There were a few hundred in attendance in a huge, tented area near his residence. I was given a seat near to him, as his guest. What followed was a religious spectacle such as I had never witnessed! The passion of his followers, who completely looked upon the Sheikh for their spiritual guidance and path to heaven, was unbelievable. Such is their deep loyalty that they are prepared to follow almost any of his directions. His 'soldiers' or disciples chanted holy scriptures and performed self-flagellation as they danced. The atmosphere was incredible as the stomping of feet rose to a crescendo. The spectacle was both scary and bewildering to me as a newcomer. The hours slipped by and after about four hours we shared a delightful meal at the Sheikh's house. The memory is still so vivid. It is my belief that if only the whole world could witness this religious fervour and deep belief in God, a change can be affected, and people can see that the Moslem faith and its many facets is truly a religion of peace. Sheikh Mansour Diouf was interviewed by Seog Byung Kim in September 2017 and asked: "*When you are in Mrs. Moon's presence, how do you perceive her?*"

His detailed answer is a wonderful testimony to True Mother:

"*I see in her the great scholars of Islam, the feminine aspect. The Qur'an often recalls Muhammad's first wife Khadija, who was wise and helped, supported, and understood him. She was not an ordinary person. When I think of Sheikh Amadou Bamba, I think of his mother, Mame Diarra Bousso, who sacrificed herself for him, for humanity and who gave her life. She died at the age of thirty-three, the same age as Jesus. When I see Dr. Moon, I also think of the Virgin Mary. I think of all those great women in the Qur'an whom God praised. They have laid the foundations of a pure humanity, a healthy humanity. When I see Mrs. Moon, I see that kind of person. All that she does is prescribed by Islam. Unfortunately, Islam remains unknown. It is a religion of peace that demands that we love our neighbour, that we sacrifice for the sake of others, that we see others as better than ourselves. This is what she does – helping people, sacrificing, giving herself, praying for them, and so on. For me, she is a true leader for Islam. I take this opportunity to say that today Islam needs it. If I understand correctly, she did not come for a religion, she came for everybody. Since she came for everybody, I want her to know that Islam is part of this everybody. Islam has a bad image, which everyone knows, the image of a religion of terror, war, and terrorism. No, this is not Islam. The true Islam of the Qur'an, dictated by Prophet Muhammad, is Islam that advocates peace, development, the communion of hearts with God. Today, I believe that the action she has taken other communities must also carry out. I see all the communities here – yellow people, black people, white people, Catholics, Protestants. I think this is the moment to think of Islam. She should help the pacification of the Islamic world."*

During the preparations for the summit in Johannesburg on 7 December 2019, several of us were invited to have breakfast with True Mother in her suite. During the meal we were each asked to share our testimony. When it came to my turn I stood up and burst into tears as I poured out my heart. I described my course from joining the church in the spring of 1972 at the age of nineteen, to becoming a missionary to Zambia in 1975, to my then mission as the Special Envoy to South Africa. True Mother listened very intently. I felt too inadequate, unworthy, sinful, and imperfect to be a disciple. As I sat down, True Mother looked at me and said: "*We have to prepare our legacy*".

And this is my legacy – my memoirs.

My motivation is a desire to let the world know that True Parents are here; the Divine Principle is here; the Blessing is here.

I pray that people all over the world can open their spiritual eyes and see that for each one there is an opportunity to participate in the Providence of God, our Heavenly Parent.

July 2019, Morning run with President Lungu of Zambia, Kitwe, Zambia.

Glossary

Note on the language and terms used in this book.

I write as a Unificationist missionary, using the terms and expressions I have been using all my life. Many of these terms, such as 'True Parents', are deeply rooted in the life and worldview of a Unificationist. I hope that the brief explanations below can help you, my reader, catch the essence of what I have to say. But I realise that in some cases a fuller explanation will be needed.

Blessing
One of the central tenets of Unificationism is the sanctity of marriage, referred to as 'the Blessing'. Up until recently, marriage partners were suggested for each other by Rev. Moon and this was called 'the matching'; the matching is followed by the official engagement ceremony and then the wedding ceremony.

Centre
The home of a community of Unification Church members, or missionaries. Often this serves both as a place for church meetings and services and as the residence for a number of members. In such cases the community will be led by a centre leader.

Divine Principle
The principal text of Unification teachings.

FFWPU
The **Family Federation for World Peace and Unification** was established in 1994 by Reverend Sun Myung Moon. Reverend Moon stated at the founding of the FFWPU that he had never intended to create a new religion, but to open an age after religion where families would serve as the core of spiritual and character growth. [Previously, what was known as the 'Unification Church' had been established (in Korea in 1954) as the Holy Spirit Association for the Unification of World Christianity.]

Heavenly Parent
the name given to God in Unification theology

Holy Salt
used to sanctify things (similar to the use of holy water in other faiths)

Home Church
neighbourhood outreach, in particular as launched by Rev. Moon in the 1970s

Matching
See 'Blessing' above

Monsei
Celebratory cheer used in Korea to wish 10,000 years of good fortune

Movement
Unificationists use this term a lot – the Unification movement, the Zambian movement, etc. It is rooted in the concept that the Messiah does not come to found a church; this is not a denial of "church" but an expansion of the reach of God's message, so that the love of God can touch not just a believer, but a parent, a teacher, a banker, a political leader and even the policy of a nation. This is why a Unificationist missionary will find him- or herself engaged in business, education, relief work and international conferences. The same person may represent FFWPU on Sunday and UPF at a Monday conference. But it is all part of one *movement*.

Peace Embassy
In many nations a property in the capital city houses the offices of UPF. In some cases this also functions as the national headquarters for other parts of the wider movement, including FFWPU and WFWP.

Today's World
Unification Church publication for 35 years starting in 1980

True Parents
The name given to the Founders of the Holy Spirit Association for World Christianity (HSA-UWC) now known as the Family Federation for World Peace (FFWPU), Reverend Sun Myung Moon and Dr. Hak Ja Han Moon. This term is used to indicate the Messianic role as explained in Divine Principle.

True Father
Reverend Moon (see also True Parents, above)

True Mother
Dr. Hak Ja Han Moon, also known as the Mother of Peace (see also True Parents, above)

Unification Community
This term has been used in a similar way to *movement* (see above), but with a focus on Unificationists involved in a wide range of activities but residing in the same location or nation. A more recent and more generally embracing term is ***'Heavenly Parent's Holy Community'*,** which emphasises more than ever the idea that we – humanity – are all one family under the One God.

Universal Peace Federation (UPF)
Founded in 2005 by Rev. Dr. Sun Myung Moon and Dr. Hak Ja Han Moon, is a global network of individuals and organizations dedicated to building a world of peace in which everyone can live in freedom, harmony, cooperation and prosperity. UPF is an NGO in general consultative status with the Economic and Social Council of the United Nations.

Witness
to introduce someone to the Unification Church, and especially to its main teaching, the Divine Principle

Printed in Great Britain
by Amazon

64769647R00078